Scottish Novels of the Second World War

Isobel Murray

WP
BOOKS

Published by Word Power Books 2011
43–45 West Nicolson Street
Edinburgh EH8 9DB
www.word-power.co.uk

Printed and bound in Scotland
Designed by Leela Sooben

British Library Cataloguing in Publication Data.
A catalogue record for this book is available from
the British Library.

ISBN 978-0-9566283-1-2

The publisher acknowledges subsidy
from Creative Scotland towards the publication of this volume.

ALBA | CHRUTHACHAIL

CONTENTS

INTRODUCTION

We cannot consider the literary products of the Second World War as if the First War had never been. We must start, however briefly, with the impact made on populations and artists by the First. The effects of the so-called Great War were deep, wide, permanent, and by no means confined to those who were killed, wounded or bereaved. It was the end of so much: traditions, conventions, faiths, beliefs, certainties, securities. It left a great chasm between generations. A fine personal account of this was given by Naomi Mitchison to Elizabeth Haldane, her 'Aunt Bay', scholar, author, and the first Scottish woman to become a Justice of the Peace. In 1928, Mitchison wrote to her aunt, 'something of a role model for Naomi', as follows:

> I don't believe you realise how much the war has upset our
> generation – mine and the one immediately after it ....
> The first wave of disturbance was the one at the time, and
> now we're in for the second, after the period of calm and
> exhaustion immediately following the thing. I think this was
> much what happened after the Peloponnesian and after the
> Napoleonic Wars. Our's [sic]was worse than either. You have
> still a balance in your life: all that incredible pre-war period
> when things seemed in the main settled, just moving solidly

and calmly like a glacier towards all sorts of progress. But we
have had the bottom of things knocked out completely, we
have been sent reeling into chaos and it seems to us that none
of your standards are either fixed or necessarily good because
in the end they resulted in the smash-up. We have to try and
make a world for ourselves, basing it as far as possible on love
and awareness, mental and bodily, because it seems to us that
all the repressions and formulae, all the cutting off of part of
our experience, which perhaps looked sensible and even right
in those calm years, have not worked. Much has been taken
from us, but we will stick like fury to what is left, and lay
hold on life, as it comes to us. [1]

Mitchison here seems to speak for a generation or more. Her
determination to 'make a (new) world for ourselves' may be personal,
but her account of the war's effects will serve generally. There simply
could not be an equal psychological cataclysm for those (including
Mitchison herself, of course) who had to face another war twenty
years later. And among Scottish novelists who also had to live
through a Second World War were Eric Linklater, Bruce Marshall
and Compton Mackenzie. Others born later shared the shock, as
history and literature both demonstrate. They tended to be more
questioning, more educated: and they had fewer certainties to
destroy. Commentators on the Second World War seem generally
agreed that Britons entered it with less enthusiasm, less caring about
King, Country or Empire, less patriotism and religious fervour, less
belief in a cause, less conviction of an end worth fighting for: for
many, their conviction that it was a Just War was retrospective.

This book looks at how some Scottish novelists confronted the
Second World War, the biggest or second biggest happening of their
lifetimes. It would be absurd to try to generalise from the novelists of
our small country as to the nature or importance of their responses:
Scotland is too small a nation, and the fields of war are too vast for
any such arithmetical conclusion. I want to see what kinds of novel
they wrote, and then concentrate on those I think are best, or most
successful, or best deserve to survive. But I have read as widely as I

could, among my chosen field, which includes authors who were adult during the war, and who wrote about it, in military or civilian life, however long after the event. Of course it is often an accident which would-be or might-be novelists survived the war, who wrote fiction as opposed to memoirs, or histories of facets of the bigger picture, who found publishers. Even then, some novels have disappeared almost without trace.

And the war was going to be dreadful beyond all expectation. Here is the start of Martin Gilbert's *Second World War*:

> The Second World War was among the most destructive conflicts in human history; more than forty-six million soldiers and civilians perished, many in circumstances of prolonged and horrifying cruelty. During the 2174 days of war between the German attack on Poland in September 1939 and the surrender of Japan in August 1945, by far the largest number of those killed, whether in battle or behind the lines, were unknown by face or name except to those few who knew or loved them; yet in many cases, perhaps also numbering in the millions, even those who might in later years have remembered a victim were themselves wiped out. Not only forty-six million lives, but the vibrant life and livelihood which they had inherited, and might have left to their descendants, were blotted out: a heritage of work and joy, of struggle and creativity, of learning, hopes and happiness, which no one would ever inherit or pass on. [2]

His quiet, accurate, systematic account of the war, in all its fields, with its lists of deaths, victims, prisoners, is often hard to read. And on his last page he says:

> No one has been able to calculate the number of wounded, certainly amounting to several millions, whose lives were permanently scarred as a result of the war. Physical scars, from the severest disability to disfiguring wounds, and mental scars, accompanied these millions for the rest of

their lives. Many died as a direct result of them. Others lived in pain, discomfort, fear or remorse. For those civilians who were fortunate to survive privation, deportation and massacre, similar scars, physical, mental and spiritual, remained – and still remain – to torment them. The greatest unfinished business of the Second World War is human pain. (p 747)

Paul Fussell in his *Wartime* is only one of the most outspoken of modern commentators. He dismisses retrospective descriptions of the Good, or Necessary or Justified War that take awareness of the Holocaust for granted:

Both civilians and soldiers were right to perceive in the war, as Dwight Macdonald has said, 'the maximum physical devastation accompanied by the minimum of human meaning.' It takes some honesty, even if that honesty arises from despair, to perceive that some events, being inhuman, have no human meaning. [3]

This Introductory chapter looks at some of the interesting or typical novels that did not make my final eight, but combine to form a kind of picture of the Scottish response to all-out war. I decided to omit Neil Gunn's *The Green Isle of the Great Deep* (1944) on the ground that its fable is essentially a criticism of totalitarianism, rather than a book about the Second World War. I include novels by pacifists, conscientious objectors, civilians and armed services: all experienced the war, and some record their experience in novels, memoirs *and* military histories – Eric Linklater is a case in point here. And first I want to point briefly to some who were writing warnings or prophecies in the thirties, most of them very conscious of the political ferment of the times. Ian Macpherson, Highland novelist, is less political than most. His *Wild Harbour* (1936) foresees a war in about 1944. His hero Hugh plans simply to escape the inevitable. He will not fight in a war, but is unwilling to face what he foresees as the abuse that will be directed at conscientious objectors, so he and Terry plan to live out the war in the wild, stocking a cave with provisions and refusing to face the events. Inevitably he regrets his 'escape' in the end, and again it seems inevitable they die in the end, but most of the book is about the projected escape.

The more politically-minded novelists uttering warnings about the rise of Fascism and dealing also with Communism or Socialism include, of course, Lewis Grassic Gibbon in his 1934 *Grey Granite*. They also include Naomi Mitchison in *We Have Been Warned* (1935), which predicts a bloody Fascist revolution in Britain. And James Barke's *Major Operation* (1936) has clear prophecies about Fascism and war. It was dramatised in 1941, and mainly concerns the conversion of a middle-class hero to the cause of the workers, while his *Land of the Leal* (1939) is a family saga where at the end one brother goes to fight in Spain in the Civil War, while the other, a Christian minister, swithers about duty and conscience. So, particularly in the case of these forerunners, it is clear that the 'message' is more urgent than in the general run of peacetime novels, and all the traditional questions about the right or duty of the novelist to preach or persuade, about his or her sustained distance from characters or events, take new forms.

In books about the war itself, these questions continue to arise, and may in some cases help to account for the passing of many years between the experience to be recorded or recreated and the completion of the book. Sometimes the traditional difference between novel and memoir is blurred even then: George MacDonald Fraser, who spawned the Flashman novels in light-hearted historical fiction, and set the comic adventures of Private McAuslan, 'the dirtiest soldier in the British army', in postwar times, never wrote a novel about World War Two. But his masterly memoir of the war in Burma, *Quartered Safe Out Here* (1992) is outstanding. It is subtitled 'A Recollection of the War in Burma', and has its own message. He writes that war is 'not a matter of maps with red and blue arrows and oblongs, but of weary, thirsty men with sore feet and aching shoulders wondering where they are.' (xii) In particular he focuses on the war in Burma:

> A huge foreign legion of what Atlee called 'the scrapings of
> the barrel' from half the nations under the sun, fighting under

> one of the great captains in mountain, jungle, and dry plain,
> in hot sun and drenching monsoon, and inflicting on one of
> the great warrior races its most crushing defeat. (xiii)

His is a straightforwardly emotional account of the men and their
fellowship:

> I want to set down, before night, how they went to war, how
> they spoke and thought, how they were armed and dressed,
> how they fought and lived and died, and how they beat the
> living daylights out of Jap. (xvi)

But this accomplished novelist does not hesitate to use the techniques
of the novel to portray his experience, and he produces 'actual'
dialogue between his characters some forty years later without feeling
the need to apologise.

The Home Guard:
COMPTON MACKENZIE AND NIGEL TRANTER

There are two accomplished Scottish novels centred on the Home
Guard (originally the Local Defence Volunteers), and both were
published during the war. This necessitated, for each writer, a positive
outcome for the sake of morale, and a certain amount of comedy in
the writing, to keep the readers' spirits up on the home front. The
first, published in 1943, is from well-established writer Compton
Mackenzie. *Keep the Home Guard Turning* is a neat parody of the
popular song, 'Keep the Home Fires Burning'. Mackenzie had fought
in the Great War, and was 'obsessed by the folly which had permitted
another war to begin'. He wrote to his mother in spring 1940, 'I
cannot see this war as anything except a crime against man and a sin
against God.' At sixty, unable to find any war-related employment,
he retired to the island of Barra, which he had made his home in
July 1940, and was invited to take over the Local Defence Volunteers,

shortly to be redesignated the Home Guard. As his biographer Andro Linklater comments, 'To stave off Armageddon with a platoon of elderly islanders amid a blizzard of top secret and most confidential instructions from military authorities could lead only to despair or comedy.' [4] His experiences of absurdity with the Home Guard led inevitably to the third novel in his series of Ben Nevis novels, familiar to modern television viewers from the long-running *Monarch of the Glen* series.

Keep the Home Guard Turning is rich in absurdities, many of which reflected the realities of adapting the Home Guard ethos to the realities of island life. 'Monty' plays it for laughs throughout. The second chapter, 'To arms, Great Todday!' sets the mood: the poster reads,

> ## TO ARMS!
> ## MEN OF TODDAY, SHOW HITLER
> ## WHERE HE GETS OFF!

And underneath this stirring invitation was a picture in extremely vivid colours of a kilted warrior plunging a bayonet into what was intended to represent a German soldier, though perhaps on account of the speed with which the artist had worked the figure represented rather a deep-sea diver in the uniform of a postman. The appearance of this picture on the doors of the schools in Bobanish, Watasett, and Garryboo caused a rumour to spread that Mr Waggett was exhibiting a picture 'fillum' of the war, and the lorries that served these outlying populations were crowded to capacity in consequence. (p 9)

The outcome of such a meeting under Paul Waggett, the blustering and bumptious Paul Waggett, is saved only by Roderick MacRurie, 'the uncrowned king of the island', moving into English to end his Gaelic address:

> For the benefit of those poor souls who through no fault of their own cannot speak the tongue spoken by Attam and Eve in the Garden of Eden I will now say a few words in English. We are proud to find that our friend Mr Waggett is taking the grand responsibility to put the two Toddays in a suitable condition to beat off the enemy from our shores. We are crateful to him for the splendid manner in which he has answered the call of duty. We do not know if the Chermans will come to Snorvig, but if they do come, for once in a way we will not show them the hospitality we like to show our visitors. They will receive another kind of a Highland welcome altogether. It'll be warrum enough, oh yess, by Chinko, it'll be so warrum that they'll be glad to chump pack into the sea to make themselves cool. (p 17)

There follows a genial comedy in which there are exercises between the platoons of Great and Little Todday, and one of them cheats, and then the two combine in opposition to Ben Nevis, over the overweening matter of a missing left boot.

At twenty-nine, Nigel Tranter was becoming established as a writer when war broke out, and he was offered a post in RAF intelligence. He was also engaged in some insurance work, which for a time exempted him from service. He joined the Home Guard. In 1942 he became an Army private, and was sent to the Officer Cadet Training Unit (OCTU). His war thereafter was confined to Great Britain, although his biographer Ray Bradfield comments that after years of scrambling over Scottish hills, 'He came to the Army fully equipped to join the partisans or the maquis.' [5] When he turned to writing about the Home Guard, he portrayed the antics of a pedantic superior as ridiculous, but did not ridicule the whole organisation, as Mackenzie had done. In *Delayed Action*, published in 1944, his hero David Scott is an ex-soldier who lost an arm between St Valery and

Dunkirk, and now effectively runs the platoon. As in Mackenzie's novel, his superior is made absurdly formal and rule-bound, but, luckily, lazy and often absent. His men are described with cheerful comedy, but also with respect:

> Jacky Pringle and two other corporals sprang from rigid At Ease to comparatively easy Attention, sloped their rifles, and marched out into the middle of the road – and each did it differently. Jacky, the farm grieve, plodded stolidly; Archie Weir, a shepherd, paced with the high long stride of the hills – one could almost see the stick that should have accompanied him; and Andrew Kerr, who was a tractor-driver and mechanic with the Ministry of Agriculture, and the man in the unit who took his soldiering most seriously, marched out with the snap and precision of the Guards. As they fell in, one behind another, and Ordered Arms, the sergeant eyed the first two with a sort of resigned sorrow, and the last with the satisfaction of a schoolmaster for his dux on prize day. (p 22)

The men play crucial if subordinate parts in the action; they too could have been partisans or maquis.

The action involves a suspicious-looking big house in the Borders where Scott's family has farmed for generations. Scott's wife suspects German spies, and her suspicion seems gradually to be justified; the first half of the novel leads up to a confrontation with the men at Blackshaws, with the discovery that they are refugee Polish scientists, engaged on research to help the Allies. The statutory mystery foreign woman has her place too. No sooner has this been established than another man comes to 'help' them, and he turns out to be the avenging Nazi. The Border exercise of kidnap, chase and encirclement makes for a good wartime adventure with an upbeat ending.

Three stories of the sea:
ALISTAIR MACLEAN, JAMES WOOD, OSWALD WYND

The best known of all Scottish novels of the last war is of course
HMS Ulysses (1955) by Alistair MacLean (1922–87). A minister's son
brought up in Inverness-shire, MacLean joined the Royal Navy at
eighteen in 1941, and spent two and a half years at sea. Famously,
his book was panned by reviewers but sold and sold and sold. We
can ask why. It was a first novel with many faults, but in 1955 it
satisfied a need to remember and wonder at the feats of war, here
the heroic endurance of the ship's crew that battled from Scapa
Flow to Murmansk early in 1943 with vital war materials for the
embattled Russians. Importantly, the stakes are very high. Something
made it irresistible, despite the criticisms of the reviewers and the
novel's obvious flaws. Perhaps it was the underlying note of truth, the
authenticity of an author writing about his own experiences. It is a
novel of extremes – cold, fear, suspense, lack of sleep – all the crew
are exhausted from a previous mutinous sailing before the action even
starts. Its characters are all at extremes: the Captain is compared to
a saint, Peter, or Francis or the Venerable Bede; the wise doctor to
Socrates, and the Neanderthal, trouble-making stoker is described
as ape-like. The writing is often too wordy, and can embarrass itself
easily, as here. Monstrous weather strikes:

> Its claws were hurtling rapiers of ice that slashed across a
> man's face and left it welling red: its teeth were that sub-
> zero wind, gusting over 120 knots, that ripped and tore
> through the tissue paper of Arctic clothing and sunk home
> to the bone: its voice was the devil's orchestra, the roar of a
> great wind mingled with the banshee shrieking of tortured
> rigging, a requiem for fiends: its weight was the crushing
> power of the hurricane wind that pinned a man helplessly to
> a bulkhead, fighting for breath, or flung him off his feet to
> crash in some distant corner, broken-limbed and senseless.
> Baulked of prey in its 500-mile sweep across the frozen
> wastes of the Greenland ice-cap, it goaded the cruel sea

into homicidal alliance and flung itself, titanic in its energy, ravenous in its howling, upon the cockleshell that was the *Ulysses*. (pp 87-8)

Alistair MacLean never wrote as uncontrolledly again. He learned from his mistakes. MacLean made the *Guinness Book of Records* as the man who 'between 1955 and 1978 wrote 35 books of which the sales of 18 have exceeded a million copies and thirteen have been filmed'.[6] But the later best-sellers were never so overwritten and clotted: he developed an economy of plot and style that stood him in good stead. He was modest and unpretentious, preferring the phrase 'adventure story' to the word novel, and 'storyteller' to novelist. In the end no one can take away the overwhelming popular success of this supreme story-teller.

There are two other Scottish sea stories here that are less well known. These are James Wood's *The Sealer* (1959) and Oswald Wynd's *The Forty Days* (1972). James Wood, born in 1918, was educated at Robert Gordons College, Aberdeen, and served in the Army throughout World War Two. He set about creating a writing career for himself, using his experiences at sea and on land, using his hobbies of fishing and things mechanical. He rarely wrote about World War Two, as he liked his novels to remain abreast of current events. His first novel, *Northern Mission*, (1954), dealt with adventures during the protection of a remote atomic reactor. Luckily for our present purposes, his third, *The Sealer* (1958) does make use of the war, and has a well-calculated and unusual setting, in the South Atlantic. It will be remembered that the German pocket-battleship the *Graf Spee* created devastation in the South Atlantic by sinking three British merchant ships in five days before three British cruisers finally chased her into Uruguay, where her captain scuttled her in December 1939. Here Wood chooses to create a 'successor' to the *Graf Spee,* hiding among the islands of Tierra del Fuego, and supplied by a number of neutral-looking freighters.

Wood's narrator, James Fraser, is a hardened seaman, used to poaching inside the Three Mile Limit before the war, torpedoed on his first transatlantic convoy during it, and enrolled as a spy on a sheep farm in Chile to search for the piratical German ship, the *Seeadler*. His novel is tautly written, economic and effective, a good war story. But Oswald Wynd's *The Forty Days* (1972) is more ambitious, and has more profound and complex purposes, as befits the work of a writer who was brought up in Japan, and is concerned with the contrasting cultures and mindsets of his characters. It is based on historical fact. In September 1943 the elderly freighter *Oshima Maru* sailed out of Singapore with twelve hundred prisoners, mostly British, packed into her two holds. She was to make the run to Yokohama in forty days. Wynd deals with prisoner experience sensitively, although occasionally his use of language makes the reader aware of his bilingualism:

> Out in the hold the pairing off of men was marked again, marriages of convenience without sex, protection against those moments when all real living seemed lost for ever, the humanly familiar behind a dropped steel curtain that would never rise again. There was a waking in the night to utter loneliness, the thought of keeping going through another day making no sense at all, the temptation just to let yourself get on that slide which could steepen so quickly into death. And then there was old George within inches, his mouth open, making the familiar noises in his sleep which sounded like a hen calling her chicks. He was real. (p 75)

Through three characters the author investigates the clash of cultures, and through conditions of hunger and airlessness, typhoon, amoebic dysentery, torpedoes. Bill Hughes is Senior British Officer in one hold (though not a professional soldier), Major Hirado is a proud military aristocrat in the Samurai tradition, and Mike Warren, like Wynd himself of British birth and Japanese upbringing, acts as interpreter, with problems of his own. After the war, Hughes pursues Hirado with revengeful hatred. He has to report unfavourably on Warren too, to prevent his helping Hirado, who is shown to be humane within the tramlines of his beliefs. Hirado is hanged; Hughes becomes a successful hotel-chain owner, and Warren, appropriately, a reporter. Nearly thirty years after the events portrayed, this novel presents a very thoughtful picture by the novelist, who himself served in British Intelligence, and spent over three years as a prisoner of the Japanese.

Going for Coverage:
CATHERINE GAVIN AND JAMES ALLAN FORD

One of the most ambitious attempts to 'cover' part of the war, the French experience, is given in a trilogy of novels by Catherine Gavin, *Traitor's Gate* (1976), *None Dare Call It Treason* (1978) and *How Sleep The Brave* (1980). Gavin, born in Aberdeen in 1907, had a distinguished academic career before turning to journalism, and was later a war correspondent. Her chief academic interest was French history, and she wrote series of novels about nineteenth-century France, and about the Great War, before this trilogy. The story follows the war careers of two cousins. These are Mike Marchand, a record-breaking pilot who fights brilliantly with the RAF in the desert, and dies in a revenge-attack over Corsica, and Jacques Brunel, who, like Marchand, distrusts de Gaulle and avoids the Free French, choosing instead to run an independent partisan unit in the south of France.

The novels are unified by their concentration on France, and the brilliant conveying of atmosphere, and the suspense everywhere, particularly with regard to Brunel. The trilogy is unusual also in the way the author behaves: she introduces herself as a minor character (with a detestation of de Gaulle) at the start of *Traitor's Gate*, and as narrator she continues the attack relentlessly throughout, her two heroes both echoing her point of view. The General's ambition and pomposity are lambasted. Flora Alexander says that her case is 'that for many French people there was an alternative, that of resisting "as a free group, bound to no general, bound by no oath"'.[7] The author returns in the final chapter of the trilogy, when Churchill took the salute in Paris in 1944. Again she makes no attempt to disguise her feelings about de Gaulle:

> I hated him, yes I hated him that day and always, for the
> monstrous campaign of bullying, broken promises and
> emotional blackmail which had carried him, for however
> short a time, to power, and for his enmity to those who
> had helped to raise him up. I hated him for his attempts to
> increase his own prestige in France by playing rough with
> the British and the Americans. (p 307)

It is hardly appropriate to complain about slanted writing from an author as open as this about her feelings! And given that the weakest points in the trilogy seem to me to be the idealised romantic heroines, she emerges as one of her own most convincing woman characters.

James Allan Ford also 'covered' his own war experience, short in the hopeless battle for Hong Kong, long in Japanese prison camp thereafter. Ford was born in Auchtermuchty in 1920, and started at Edinburgh University before serving with the Royal Scots. After the war he was a career civil servant, who became Registrar General for Scotland. He retired in 1979, and died in 2009. *The Brave White Flag* (1961) uses his experiences as a young officer sent to defend Hong Kong against overwhelming odds, a situation dramatic enough. In both the novels arising from his own experience, Ford conveys the scene and situation scrupulously with clear, vivid prose and understated dialogue. Then he constructs a plot which informs and deepens the issues. In *The Brave White Flag* the plot concerns young Morris's relations with his platoon, and his unspoken need to satisfy or replicate his idea of 'the formidable Captain Craig'. Morris starts with 'boyish eagerness' to play the soldier, while Craig is secretly bitter: he 'could not ignore the muddled thinking and arrogant assumptions that were condemning the garrison to a bitter, hopeless struggle.' (p 37) He is alone with 'the heresy of commonsense.' Morris makes mistakes with good intentions, and at one stage unwittingly aids the Allied cause. This pivotal relationship holds the novel together, even after Morris is wounded and dies, and Craig is wounded, but will live, 'in his tormented silence'. (p 317)

Ford did not publish his novel of the eighteen-day war until twenty years later, after the official history of the campaign by Augustus Muir had been published. His novel of his own years in Japanese prison camps is further inspired by the treatment of his brother by the Japanese: this heroic brother smuggled medicines for the sick into his prison camp, and was planning a mass breakout when he was betrayed, tortured and executed. All of this is fed into *Season of Escape* (1963), a taut and atmospheric novel of men ground down by defeat, despair and desperate clinging to survival. Again Ford creates a plot, centring on the fictitious character Keir, whose wounded arm causes him to be dropped from an escape plan he had projected. Keir bears a certain resemblance to Craig in *The Brave White Flag*, both men of high personal principles and individual integrity, different from the mass. The justification of escape in the face of certain reprisals becomes a central issue, as does that of smuggling in medicines for the sick. In the end, Keir suffers torture and death, protecting his fellows: after sixty-seven days on remand, they are brought to trial, and Keir takes the responsibility so that he receives the only death sentence. The ending is low key:

> Keir, in the condemned cell, let himself sink into a torpid, almost timeless state. There was, at last, nothing left for him to do but listen to the rain and fall asleep. At last, he could fully acknowledge the weakness of his starved and maltreated body, the exhaustion of his emotions, the intolerable strain that he had imposed upon his will. He could accept himself without question. He did not need to do any more thinking about anything. He knew all that he needed to know. (p 281)

War in a longer view:
BRUCE MARSHALL AND JACK RONDER

This war can also be treated as part of the conspectus of a novel or family saga covering a longer period: Bruce Marshall's *The Black Oxen* (1972) and *Only Fade Away (1954)* both cover their respective heroes' experiences in both wars, plus of course the times in between.

The war experience in Europe in both wars is vividly and unpleasantly rendered; not surprisingly, for Marshall was a good novelist and an experienced soldier. A Roman Catholic convert, Marshall wrote entertaining works on religious matters, from *Father Malachi's Miracle* (1931), to *The World, the Flesh, and Father Smith* (1946), and *Father Hilary's Holiday* (1965) to *Marx the First* (1975). But the two novels that stretch over two wars are perhaps more immediately accessible to the secular reader, and Marshall had a fine war record. His student days at St Andrews were interrupted by World War One. He served – and lost a leg – in the Irish Fusiliers. In World War Two the loss of his leg prevented active service in the field, but he was in the Intelligence Division of the British Army throughout.

Only Fade Away has a vague general likeness to Waugh's war trilogy *Sword of Honour* and like Waugh's Guy Crouchback, his hero is unheroic and constantly caring in selfish ways about his own perfection or reputation more than the war itself. He wears a monocle, and is rather absurd, but he is pursued over the years by a certain Hermiston, who bullied him at school, and who crops up to scupper him time after time. The reader is gradually made to sympathise, despite the absurdity.

Another longer chronological treatment is Jack Ronder's family saga, *The Lost Tribe* (1978). Ronder (1924-1979) is technically perhaps too young for a mention here; and a boy at the start, he later had a reserved occupation as a scientist. But this novel has a particular interest, in the context of the Second World War. It is a fictionalised life of Ronder's Jewish grandfather. Moshe escaped pogroms in Lithuania and attempted to reach the USA, but was consigned instead to a hard life in Dundee. He went back for his former sweetheart, and they began a long, wretched, poverty-stricken marriage, raising six children in cold, damp tenement housing. The children are all prone to tuberculosis. When the First World War starts, those among them eligible for combat have no compunction about dodging the fight. Moshe was a very faithful Jew, but Ronder traces the disintegration of family and faith generally. They are horrified by news of the concentration camps, and later dream of Israel. By the end, Moshe's grandson David is the only survivor prospering: he loses his faith, and goes to World War Two as a Scot, rather than a Jew. At the end he visits Moshe with his gentile partner and baby son: Moshe dies rejecting his grandson, and David sees that the young family of three are already *in* the 'Promised Land', as accepted members of society, 'until you could no longer pick them out'. Well written and illuminating, *The Lost Tribe* is worth seeking out.

The Lure of Hemingway:
NEIL PATERSON/JOHN KOVACK

Neil Paterson (1916-1995) was born in Greenock and attended Edinburgh University. He was to go on to publish *The China Run* (1948) and *Behold Thy Daughter* (1950), and contribute greatly to Scotland's film and theatre culture, but his first novel *On my Faithless Arm* was published in 1946 under the *nom de plume* of John Kovack. He served in minesweepers 1940-6. A creditable first novel, it suffers somewhat from an overdose of Hemingway. The dialogue in particular, short, simple and (hopefully) resonant, could often be lifted from *A Farewell to Arms* (1929). It is the love story of two Americans who are united after a long engagement apart when Jane arrives in London in 1941. She has ideals about helping the war effort, but her foreign correspondent husband-to-be has been living in London and having an affair with English Stella, and drinking far too much. Here the war is genuinely present, and Mick knows plenty about it. Like a Hemingway hero, Mick can be a nasty drunk, and is determined not to love Stella:

> I knew we still had a reckoning to come and I did not care where we went to have it. I wasn't worrying about that or about anything else. I was through with worrying. And I was through with thinking. And most of all I was through with fighting. I wanted one thing only. I wanted the rain to stop. (p 36)

Jane arrives, and she and Mick marry, but the relationship is doomed. They see little of each other. In spite of Mick's opposition, she volunteers to drive an ambulance. Meantime Stella's distanced husband is horribly wounded: 'He's not dead. I think it's something worse.' (p 206) She feels bound, if she can, to stay with him. Jane's ambulance is bombed, and when she is shocked but relatively unharmed, she refuses to go home with Mick: it appears she is in love with their friend Dave, a brave pilot. Spurned, Mick goes off and on impulse joins the RAF. In the buttoned-lip style of sub-Hemingway, the last chapter is half a page. It begins, 'I did not go near London my first three leaves.' It ends with Mick revisiting a canteen in London, going up to a girl working there:

> I knew then that it had started again, and that it was all exactly as it had been before.
> "Hullo Stella," I said.

Paterson later discounted the book, but the novel remains very readable, and intent on its themes of commitment and betrayal, both to love and to war, illustrating the Auden poem from which it takes its title, 'Lullaby', 1940:

> Lay your sleeping head, my love,
> Human on my faithless arm.

Self-selected Scots:
ALLAN CAMPBELL MACLEAN AND JOHN PREBBLE

Allan Campbell MacLean, well-known children's novelist, was born in Lancashire in 1922. He adopted the Scottish Highlands as his home, and all his books save one are based in Scotland. The exception is the most 'ritually violent' of all the novels here, *The Glasshouse* (1969). [8] It chronicles the experience of its hero, who is sent to a British Army Field Punishment Centre in August 1945, just after the Hiroshima bomb. His crime: insubordination. For this he is subjected to prolonged physical and mental torture, and brutally pointless punishments. The book is a grim condemnation of war and what it does to its participants: the warders are all like our worst images of Nazis. The message is unmistakable, and the book is so unpleasantly redolent of sadism that it is hard to read.

John Prebble was also born in England, in 1915, but he was raised in Saskatchewan. Angus Calder wrote in his *Independent* obituary that 'his love affair with Highland Scotland was lifelong and constant', adding that the affair began before he ever saw Scotland. Prebble wrote two war novels, one before he had any experience of action himself, one after. It shows! Called up in 1940, he spent the early years in North Wales, where he wrote *Where the Sea Breaks* (1944) Understandably, the result is rather theoretical: German airmen are shot down on a Scottish island, where they attempt to dominate the simple, religious inhabitants, but in the end the victory, moral and realistic, is with the islanders. Prebble's second novel, *The Edge of Darkness* (1948) is much more rewarding, as it mirrors his later war experience, 'Hamburg-London, 1946'. Like Campbell MacLean, he treats the end of the war, but not exactly a victory. He produces a really interesting and thoughtful account of the attitudes of a front-line searchlight troop: 'None of them could ever be young again'. (p 130) We learn much of the easy social intimacy between soldiers, their enthusiastic looting, their shock at meeting 'real' Germans, and the utter dereliction of Hamburg. Interestingly, towards the end, two of the characters shy away from civilian life and sign up to stay in the Army in peacetime. This book is definitely worth hunting down.

World War Two and Time Travel: The Science Fiction of **ARCHIE ROY**

Twenty-five years after the end of the war, we find it used in Science Fiction, in the ingenious world of Archie Roy. Roy was born in 1924, and became Professor of Astronomy at the University of Glasgow and a founder of the Society for Psychical Research. He published six Science Fiction novels, including *All Evil Shed Away* (1970), where he makes adroit use of time travel experiments. His premise is that Germany won the war, through the assassination of Churchill and his war cabinet in 1940. Now, in 1969, Germany rules Europe and Africa, Joe McCarthy is President for life in America, and Japan rules across the Pacific, all in precarious imbalance. Each hates the others but is unable to conquer them without their own assured destruction. Someone will have to go back in time and unkill Churchill. The experiments take place on an atmospheric St Kilda, and both the island and the time travel are vividly conveyed.

Upper class Edinburgh encounters war:
WINIFRED PECK, married to a Scot

A last word for Peck, who was not a Scot, but married one, and lived in Edinburgh, at the upper end of the social scale. In 2006 Persephone Books reprinted her *House-Bound*, written and first published in 1942. It covers the early months of that year, when Rose, the mistress of a large house, decides to do without servants as her contribution to the war effort. Her husband is appalled: 'I can't have you opening the door to tradespeople!' We are not allowed to forget 'the slaughter and the agony in Europe', but otherwise in general gentle comedy is directed at the hapless Rose and her peers, and one clear note echoes throughout – 'no more service after this war', an aim which eventually becomes 'what matter if the world of the privileged and idle and cultured passed away?'

NOTES

1. See Jill Benton, *Naomi Mitchison: A Biography*, London, 1990, p 50. The 'role model' quotation is from Jenni Calder, p 3.

2. See Martin Gilbert, *Second World War,* New Edition, 2000, p 1.

3. See Paul Fussell, *Wartime: Understanding and Behaviour in the Second World War*, New York and Oxford, 1989, p 143. The Macdonald quotation is from *Memoirs of a Revolutionist*, p 96.

4. See Andro Linklater, *Compton Mackenzie: A Life*, London, 1987, pp 286, 287, 289.

5. Ray Bradfield, *Nigel Tranter: Scotland's Storyteller*, Edinburgh, 1999, p 64.

6. Norris McWhirter, ed, *Guinness Book of Records, Guinness Superlatives,* Enfield, 1981, p 97.

7. Flora Alexander, 'The Novels of Catherine Gavin', in David Hewitt, ed, *Northern Visions: Essays on the Literary Identity of Northern Scotland in the Twentieth Century*, East Linton, 1995, pp 166-78, esp p 176. Interested readers might care to compare Gavin's analysis with the more measured analysis of Vichy in Allan Massie's Saltire prize-winning novel, *A Question of Loyalties*, 1989.

8. Alan Bold, *Modern Scottish Literature*, London, p 233.

ERIC LINKLATER
and *Private Angelo*

Dates: 1899–1974.

Youth and Pre-War: Born Penarth, Wales. Raised Orkney. Went to Aberdeen University to read English.

WWI: 1918 Orderly Corporal on the Somme: 4–5 months as a private in the Black Watch: three weeks as sniper: wounded.

WW2: TA Reservist: defence of Scapa Flow. Sent to Iceland, Faeroes, etc to write on northern garrison service: also defence of Calais, 51st Highland Division etc: almost a year in Italy, writing contemporaneous war history without supervision.

Novels: *Private Angelo*, 1946; *The Dark of Summer*, 1956; *Roll of Honour*, 1961.

War-related: Several accounts of war history for the War Office; three volumes of autobiography, especially *Fanfare for a Tin Hat*, 1970.

Post-war: Prolific full-time writer in many genres.

Like Naomi Mitchison, Bruce Marshall, Compton Mackenzie and others, ERIC LINKLATER experienced two World Wars. Further he went on to report on the war in Korea, and he composed many pamphlets and histories of the Second World War. Both Wars feature at large in his three volumes of memoirs, but only the Second looms importantly in his fiction. Linklater was always aware of the distinctions he made between memoirs, histories and fiction, and was scrupulous about observing these: conversation can be 'remembered' word for word in only partially recalled memoir, or of course in fiction, but the histories are scrupulous, and although often written at the time from a partial view point, remain largely unchallenged.

Time was an important element, as the writer recognised. He tended to leave a good deal of time between the action and the writing. It is interesting that he wrote about his World War One experience as a sniper briefly in *The Man on My Back* (1941), but only expanded his analysis of his eighteen-year-old self in his last volume of memoirs, *Fanfare for A Tin Hat* (1970). In fiction, he had almost omitted any treatment of his hero's war in his first novel, *White-Maa's Saga* (1929), choosing instead to follow his young ex-soldier hero into university and early love affairs. And subsequent novels turned away to other things. It is only in *Fanfare* that he returns to this experience, reflecting on it with some maturity: he dwells on the intensity of his three weeks of killing, with a context that deals with the realities of war.

> I, a microscopic projection of general insanity, shared to
> the full its insensate purpose, and with a robust perversion
> enjoyed the brief remnant of my active service. My few
> weeks as a sniper gave to my life an excitement, an intensity,
> which I have never known since. I have, on the whole,
> had a happy life, and I have known much pleasure. But
> in my nineteenth year I lived at a high pitch of purpose, a
> continuous physical and mental alertness, that has never
> again suffused my brain and body – and which, in later
> years, my body and brain could not have sustained. [1]

The title of this volume marks the end of Linklater's brief war experience in 1918: he was hit by a German bullet which had made 'a neat little hole' in his helmet, and 'gone off in the general direction of Ypres'. (F p 11) Linklater emerged from this war with a detestation of the whole idea of war: 'intellectually intolerable'; 'an outrage against common sense'; 'abominable'; 'a landscape of incommunicable horror' – and at the same time an admiration for the fighting men of all the services, which he never lost, and which is manifest in all his treatments of war.

Linklater differed from some contemporaries in finding the possibilities of Communism as appalling as the rise of Fascism, so his view as the climate of the thirties darkened into war was desperate indeed: Spain threw him off balance, as these threatening futures faced each other in battle. He wrote novels of warning, but his rewriting of *Lysistrata* as *The Impregnable Women* (1936), a passionate denunciation of war, was, he admitted, a failure. He followed it with *Judas* (1939). He regarded 1938 as 'one of the shabbiest years of our history': this is how he regarded the way Britain and France 'made no effective protest' when Nazi Germany marched into Czechoslovakia.

But as he tells us in *Fanfare*: 'I admitted fear, I rebounded in indignation – a reversal of temper that many experienced – and presently I went to a tailor in Edinburgh and was measured for two suits of khaki.' (F p 161) As *Fanfare* describes it, at forty he was still on the lists of the Territorial Army Reserve of Officers, so was called upon to defend Scapa Flow with a meagre and ill-trained company. Like the larger country, they were 'ludicrously unprepared for war.' (F p 163) Most of his war thereafter was as a spectator, recording for the War Office a number of pamphlets about Iceland, Calais and the Highland Divisions, Italy. This could be regarded as ideal material-gathering for later fictions.

I have suggested that the most reliable and mature of Linklater's volumes of autobiography was the last written. Now I am going to choose, paradoxically, to concentrate on the most immediate of his war fictions. *Private Angelo* was begun in Rome during the writer's many months in Italy, preparing for the War Office what he himself described as a 'tedious long account of the Army' (F p

249) and finished at home in Orkney, in August 1945. No time for the maturing process I earlier advocated. More, Linklater went on to write other novels that dealt with the war: I am not spoiled for choice. The outstanding candidates are *The Dark of Summer* (1956) and *Roll of Honour* (1961).

Part of the case for *The Dark of Summer* as a major example of Linklater's fiction was made by Allan Massie in the Linklater Lecture, given in Aberdeen's WORD Festival in May 1999. Massie's favourite Linklater novel, it is certainly a rattling good yarn, that covers a lot of ground. It is probably better plotted and structured than *Private Angelo*, which, whatever the vagaries of its characters, has to follow the actual course of events in the war. It begins with the investigation of possible espionage in Finland, and leads to the memorable and gruesome recovery of a frozen corpse and its transport through storms to Shetland, where we are introduced to the strange, striking and probably sinister figure of Mungo Wishart. His private historical obsessions involve another long-lost corpse, and a family hostility dating back to Jacobite times, and eventually he can only escape these and current suspicions of treason by suicide. Meanwhile our nervous hero, Tom Chisholm, the first person narrator, briefly sees action in the Western Desert, and comes to take a dismal view of the stalled war in Italy. But his own Italian experience is mundane enough – feeding the army – 'a year of shopkeeping from the Volturno to the Gothic Line.' (p 200) Later, he is promoted to study army 'shopkeeping' in Korea, where, like Angelo earlier, he loses a left arm. By the end, the issues that perturb soldiers are those surrounding the Cold War. Chisholm insists on the personal shape of the story: 'This is not a tale of war. It is only the story of a man who, fearing and detesting war, has seen something of it.' (p 250) The romantic subplot is less than wholly successful, and the book is held together somewhat precariously by the character of the fearful soldier Chisholm. He could be said to lack a convincing distinctive individuality, while the plot could be said to be rather unnecessarily complicated.

It is opposite qualities that deter me from opting to concentrate on *Roll of Honour* (1961). It has very little plot indeed, and centres on a retired schoolmaster Andrew Birnie, who sees himself as a failure. The death of a former headmaster who had been very influential on Birnie sends him back to the old school's Roll of Honour, boys whom he had taught who perished in war, their characters and scattered deaths. Each is made individually distinct in a very particular death situation, and then set to rest again. Very moving in places, this novel, expressed at times in a sort of free verse which Linklater intended to represent 'interior monologue' or the process of remembering, vividly illustrates Linklater's devotion, already stressed, to the lives and the memories of the 'ordinary' servicemen he is celebrating. Here is a brief example, the tale of Geoffrey, whose paternity was questioned:

> He was a difficult boy,
> High-strung and clever,
> Though not quite clever enough to excuse
> His sulks and tantrums.
> But he improved with the years
> And at eighteen was good at his books,
> Popular, and fairly good at games.
> He was good enough, when the time came,
> for a commission in the Royal Tank Regiment,
> and when the battle for Rome was renewed in May,
> May 1944,
> Under the ghostly walls of the ruined abbey
> High on Monte Cassino,
> He beneath his carapace of armour
> Was early across that sinister stream
> the Rapido,
> where the first bridgehead
> was little more than a toe-hold
> in a tempest of iron hail.
> His tank was hit, bow on, by an 88-millimetre shell,
> And when there was time to count casualties
> There was nothing to distinguish his incinerated bone
> from the cindered bones
> of his driver and gunner.

Doubt as to who he was had attended his birth,
And doubt as to which he was
Returned with his death. (p 94)

So why choose to concentrate on *Private Angelo*? In the end, of
course, the choice is personal, but Linklater, always very self-aware,
outlines some of the reasons for my choice in *Fanfare for a Tin Hat*.
His memoir indicates some incidents of his own experience which
inform the novel.

The best known of these concerns Linklater's part in the discovery,
near Siena, in a country house, of many hidden treasures of the Uffizi
and the Pitti Palace in Florence, left with virtually no guardianship
to face a potential host of souvenir hunters. Linklater's reaction was
two-fold: he contacted the authorities to some effect, and ensured
that the treasures be safely guarded – and he confesses to sneaking
in by himself and kissing the flower-girls in Botticelli's *Prima Vera*.
This inspires the scene in *Private Angelo* where Angelo rushes into the
damaged castle of Pontefiore and finds the remains of the Piero della
Francesca *Adoration of the Shepherds*, mangled by the gunfire of a
German officer, and rescues and takes possession of the undamaged
head of the Virgin.

But the crucially persuasive passages of *Fanfare* describe his own
reactions to Italy, its beauty, its artistic heritage contrasting with
the ugliness of modern war. He had, as I have recorded, written a
dry account of the war in Italy, from which personal reactions were
excluded as far as possible: now, in both memoir and novel, he is
free if he so wishes to describe a love affair with a country and its
people which is everywhere informed by the circumstance of the
time, when the inevitability of eventual victory informs the whole
with elements of exhilaration which never cancel out the horrors
of war. *Private Angelo* operates as an antidote to the 'tedious long
history'.

In 1944 the writer was to report on a static war:
    Now, after a bitter winter and months of grim fighting, the
    Allies appeared to have been decisively halted under the pale

menace of Monte Cassino and before the many-gunned, thickly mined banks of the Garigliano. (F p 252)

But when he got there, 'the static war had become fluid and expansive.' (F p 267) After the fall of Rome in June, he acquired 'great freedom of movement.' (F p 272) It was in the following weeks that Linklater helped to discover and protect the great art treasures of Florence, and eventually came again to Rome, 'and there, soon after kissing Botticelli's flower-girls, I began to write the novel which became *Private Angelo*.' (F p 291) *Fanfare for a Tin Hat* remains one of the most readable volumes of memoirs I know, and it articulates a few insights no one else would have the right to assert:

> I had already given much of my heart to Italy, and now –
> though the local wine was bad – I renewed my dedication.
> I had also acquired a deep affection – born of admiration,
> nurtured by wide friendship – for the Eighth Army; and
> that also, in the weeks to come, was reinforced. I lived,
> indeed, in a state of idealistic adultery, and of that union,
> of course, *Private Angelo* was born. My emotions were taut
> as fiddle-strings, and the sober, stone-walled charm of little
> towns, the romantic enmity of the hills, and the insoluble
> virtues of our rain-drenched soldiers vibrated on them in a
> discordance I could not regret. (F pp 300-1)

So *Private Angelo* is above all a novel of contrasts, undertaken in the exhilarating knowledge that the war would soon end in Allied victory in Europe: the novel ends with the significantly noted dates of composition, 'Rome 1944 – Orkney, August 1945. It is the only successful novel I know written so soon after the events portrayed, and a significant exception to the usual rule of allowing some time for material to settle, and for the writer to establish a proper distance. It begins with the Italian surrender, signing an Armistice with the Allies (September 1943), and ends with the German Army surrendering to the Allies after their disastrous defeat on the Po (April 1945). Indeed, in the end it projects Italy a couple of years into the future, leaving Angelo and his compatriots working hard at reconstruction.

The major underlying, unequivocal contrast is between war and its destructiveness, and sexual love and its issue, its creativity. Unlikely though it seems in a Scottish novel, sex is almost everywhere celebrated as a natural positive, its indulgence, even involving unfaithfulness, is almost everywhere forgiven, and the issue, the baby, is everywhere almost immediately welcomed. The exception to the welcome is the rape of both Lucrezia and Angelo by a savage Moroccan. Angelo's fiancée Lucrezia is forgiven for having an English soldier's baby during Angelo's three-year absence at war: Angelo and Lucrezia forgive each other for the shame of rape: Angelo and Lucrezia marry soon after: Angelo is temporarily dismayed at discovering their first child is black: and Angelo brings home his pregnant mistress Annunziata with her toddler, born not to her Italian husband but the unhappy Pole Stanislas. He briefly laments his fate:

> Oh, I cannot bear it! What am I but a poor Italian soldier,
> who has done nothing wrong, unless under orders, and now
> I am expected to settle down as a married man with three
> children to care for, one of whom is an Englishman, another
> a Pole, and the third a Moor! It is too much, I say, and I
> cannot bear it! (p 249)

But soon he comes to terms with circumstances, and says to himself:

> It is possible, it even seems probable, that I have a mission.
> I must demonstrate that all the peoples of the world – or
> four of them, at least – can make their home together in
> civilization. I shall bring up these children in such a way that
> they will have no obsession about their nationality, and that
> will be a very good thing indeed. (p 250)

By the end of the novel he has become more enthusiastic. The adults have all worked very hard at regenerating the small farm, Lucrezia and Annunziata have each had another child, and each is again pregnant: now Angelo has virtually a harem, and an international nursery. (Linklater disavowed any effort toward realism in *Fanfare!*) Angelo's friend Simon Telfer revisits to meet old friends and voices grudging admiration:

> Yes, we may have been wrong about them. We laughed at them in Africa, because they ran like rabbits from time to time, but we may have been wrong. They've got something. It's their own sort of courage, but they've got it.

And Angelo, the born coward, declares at the very end, 'We have learnt the most useful of all accomplishments, which is to survive!' (p 272)

None of the sexual activity in the book is explicit, or rendered at any length, but when it comes to the destructiveness of war in contrast to all this Linklater relies in part on long descriptive passages, which are so effective that they need only happen once or twice. When the novelist directs our attention to the large-scale account of the Allies prepared to meet the Germans in a late confrontation, he shows his unusual mastery of the course of the war, and the width of the alliance. The emphasis appears simply to be on language:

> The Germans had entrenched themselves from sea to sea across the Etruscan Apennines, and against their ramparts of concrete and steel and cloud-swept hill there had striven, week by week for the advantage of another mile, the polyglot forces of democracy, born of many lands and bred to divers habits, but all alike in that all could shiver and bleed. On the left of the line, by the western sea, there had been Brazilians and American negroes, and on the right, on the Adriatic shore, Greeks and Poles. In the mountains north of Florence men had given their orders to advance, and others had cursed them, in the accents of New England

and the Middle West, in voices from the cornfields of
Kansas and the cold plains of Nebraska, from the black soil
of the deep South and the arrogant immensity of Texas.
Voices from the Transvaal and the Cape had answered
them, and to the eastward came a clamour of tongues from
Hindustan. Soldiers had died with a sentence, half-spoken,
of Urdu on their lips. They had called gently to each other
in the night in Gurkhali and Mahratti, and heard the debate
of comrades in the broad accent of Yorkshire, the lazy flow
of Cotswold villages, the quick traffic of a London borough,
and here and there the softness of Gaelic. Christchurch and
Dunedin had spoken to Glasgow and Liverpool, Manitoba
and Quebec to Warsaw and Athens. Pietermaritzburg had
conversed with Little Rock, the Grampians with the Punjab,
and tied each other's wounds.

But the novelist is not simply inviting us to wonder at the breadth of
the Alliance: unlike a majority of war novelists, he draws attention at
the end of all this to an Allied urge to violence and destruction equal
to that of the enemy:

Hardly since the confounding of the people at Babel had
such a diversity of tongues been heard, and month by
month their hopeful or their weary speech had sounded a
little farther to the north, till now, in the cold bright air of
spring, the languages and lingos, the argots and parley and
paronyms of half the world, to the orchestration of their
innumerable artillery, were shouting for the kill.[2] (pp 234-5)

In general one such long description of the destructiveness of war
also suffices: here is a composite picture of refugees in little towns
along the Appian Way:

Our age of steel and explosives had shown itself very like
the Ice Age in its ability to alter the face of a landscape,
create lacunae, and remove excrescences. Wedding-chamber

and warm kitchen, the smithy and the grocer's shop and the
notary's office had been reduced to rags and dusty rubble
by a stick of bombs that caught the sunlight as they fell.
With a huff and a puff the metallurgist and the chemist
had blown away the long toil of many simple masons, and
whole families who had spent their arduous and patient
years in the growing of corn and wine had vanished in a
little acrid smoke. A bridge that had served a thousand
needs, and many thousand brisk and busy people, and
filled its valley with arcs of beauty and proud columns,
had been demolished with boisterous success by a cartload
of guncotton... Of all the triumphs that had marched the
Appian Way none had so spaciously shown the enormity
of human power as this great spectacle of destruction; and
the pity was that the refugees could not appreciate it as it
deserved. The refugees were unimpressed by the march and
the majesty of science. (p 146)

No need to do this again for the attentive reader, until we come to the
utterly useless and mistaken destruction of Angelo's native village of
Pontefiore in a case of what nowadays is called friendly fire. Here is
just a part of the experience:

Then they heard – faintly at first, but quickly it grew louder
– a noise that was more like a sensation of feeling than of
hearing; for it rubbed upon their ears. Gleaming like beads
of ice, with the morning sun upon them, the bombers
looked very pretty under the tall arch of the sky.
    It was unfortunate that the pilots' information was not
up to date. They knew that the Germans had occupied
Pontefiore, but no one had told them that the Germans
had left it. Their bombs, that fell with great accuracy on
the chosen targets, were in fact wasted; and so indeed
was Pontefiore. A thunderstorm seemed to break upon
the little town, and from it rose fountains of rubble that
smeared the pale blue sky with grey dust. In the lower

darkness of the storm red flames began to leap, and here
and there a wooden beam or a large piece of masonry
was thrown far above the general upheaval. The roar of
the bombers, fretting eardrums, persisted through the
thunder. (p 182)

Otherwise, it is small details that underline the violence: Angelo in
a packed train supporting an oldish sleeping man who turns out to
be dead (p 55); the brutal behaviour of Captain Schlemmer, who
ends up shooting the adoring shepherds in a Piero della Francesca
Adoration; his later petty destruction of everything in the village,
down to the Countess's prized volumes of Ouida, and some harmless
outlying beehives. (pp 163-7) These are shocking, but not allowed
to dominate. However dark the scene, the novel is called a comedy,
and features many comic scenes too: the Marchesa reclining on
the hidden recumbent body of the Count during a German search
(Chapter 6), Angelo singing tunelessly to a wounded English soldier
trapped upside-down in a jeep, to keep him awake (pp 79-80); Angelo
involuntarily escaping from a vehicle, 'astride the tallest ox in the
herd.' (p 125)

With these contrasting elements always in the background, the
structure of the book is twofold. Firstly, each chapter is centred
either on Angelo, or on the Count his father, or on both, and their
various adventures give the book a comic diversity. The Count
is a somewhat devious, philosophical nobleman, pompous and
longwinded, and capable of crime and hypocrisy: he withheld the
food supplies he was to send to Africa for the Italian army – he says,
in case of bombs or shipwreck, but he kept them for himself. He
serves as custodian of culture and womaniser. Essentially, he serves
as contrast, again, to Angelo, his illegitimate son, an innocent but
acute peasant who crowns three years of inglorious war in Africa by
being the first and fastest to run away from fighting the British on
their landing at Reggio de Calabria in September 1943. The second
way of structuring the novel is Linklater's masterly plot creation,
which on the one hand has to follow the true course of the war,
and on the other has Angelo fight in turn for the Italians, until the

armistice signed that very day; then, and most unwillingly, for the Germans, until he makes his escape; next he is adopted into an English outfit with his friend Simon Telfer, who finally decides it is Angelo's duty to join the Italian troops training to fight along with the Allies against the Germans.

Into this complex and entertaining adventure tale the young Angelo goes, usually 'in a white trance of fear', undergoing all sorts of accidents, including a broken leg, homosexual rape by a Moor, and losing his left hand in battle. But it is the education of this young Candide that is the most memorable feature of the book, and his comments as he tries to make sense of the meaninglessness of war are a delight and a challenge to any reader. It is the Allied promise of liberation that most perplexes him:

> 'Excuse me,' said Angelo, 'but when I went to school in
> Siena I was taught that to liberate means to set free. Is that
> so, please?'
>   'It is,' said Michael.
> 'And in September we were told that you and the Americans
> were coming to liberate Italy.'
> 'And now we have come,' said Michael coldly.
> 'But those soldiers, who said they had liberated the turkeys
> and the geese, had taken a most drastic way of giving
> them their freedom. I do not deny that turkeys and geese,
> especially in winter, lead a very dull and disagreeable and
> apprehensive life. So do many human beings, however, and
> if the Allies have decided that all who are unfortunate can
> be liberated only by wringing their necks –'
> 'I'm afraid I can't spend the whole day gossiping,' said
> Michael, and stood up. 'I have work to do.' (p 86)

Angelo asks another soldier, 'Would you say that this village had been liberated?' and gets the reply, 'Oh, properly liberated. There isn't a roof left in it.' (p 87) Twelve miles from Cassino Angelo and Simon are hit by 'friendly fire', and Angelo is unwilling to accept Simon's assurance, 'We all make mistakes from time to time.' He replies, 'We do not all carry bombs. To make a private mistake in your own house is one thing, but to make a public mistake with a bomb of two hundred and fifty kilogrammes is different altogether.' (p 95)

Two years before *Private Angelo* was published, Mitchison had a similar thought. In her diary on 16 June 1944 she wrote: 'I keep wondering how much people in Normandy *want* to be liberated. I mean, having their farms burnt and cattle killed and everything.' Paul Fussell ponders again in 1989: 'The world was laughing at Italy, and yet the Italians were sensibly declining to be murdered.' [3]

Angelo's apprehension grows. Seeing the flow of refugees along the Appian Way, he says,

> 'All these people have been liberated and now they have
> nowhere to live. And before the war is over you will have
> to liberate northern Italy and France, and Greece and
> Yugoslavia, and Holland and Belgium, and Denmark and
> Poland and Czechoslovakia.'
> 'It may take us rather a long time,' said Simon.
> 'And when you have finished no one in Europe will have
> anywhere to live.'
> 'You mustn't exaggerate. It won't be as bad as that.'
> '*Speriamo*,' said Angelo. (p 147)

Simon accuses him of becoming tiresome when he goes on, 'We are very grateful to you for coming to liberate us, but I hope you will not find it necessary to liberate us out of existence.' (p 148) Occasionally, because of Angelo's very innocence, the narrator has to take a hand in puncturing some clichés or satirising the English officer. Simon Telfer belongs to an elite and irregular British force:

> To join and remain in Force 69 it was necessary that an
> officer should be naturally brave, uncommonly resourceful
> and know a great number of people by their Christian
> names... Simon Telfer knew at least three hundred. (p 82)

As he gains some insights, Angelo has become fractionally less afraid and a bit more knowing. Eventually he preaches a mini sermon about liberation to an audience of three women, two of them listening indulgently but unbelieving, the third just anxious to flee. The effect on his audience is rather to undermine his peasant wisdom, and his eloquence begins to remind us of the Count his father:

> In the first place, before a town or village can be liberated
> it must be occupied by the Germans, and the Germans
> will rob it of everything they can find; but that is of
> no importance, that is merely the Overture. Liberation
> really begins when the Allied forces bomb the town: that
> is the First Movement, *Allegro*, so to speak. The Second
> Movement is often quite leisurely but full of caprice: it
> occurs when the Allied artillery opens fire to knock down
> what the bombers have missed, and may be called *Andante
> Capriccioso*. After that has gone on for some time the
> liberating infantry will rush in, that is the Third Movement,
> the *Scherzo*, and though the Allied soldiers do not loot, of
> course, they will find a number of things such as geese and
> hens and wine, that apparently belong to no one – for the
> local inhabitants have taken to the hills or are hiding in their
> cellars - and to prevent the wine and the geese from being
> wasted, the soldiers will naturally take care of them. Then
> comes the Last Movement, when the officials of the Allied
> Military Government arrive and say to the inhabitants, 'No,
> you cannot do that, you must go there, you are not allowed
> to sell this, and you are forbidden to buy that. If you want
> to live here you must apply for our permission, and it is
> against the law for you to be domiciled anywhere else.' Yes,
> that is the *Finale*, and then you may say that the process of
> liberation is complete. (pp 179-80)

It is very easy, then, to read *Private Angelo* as not only of the lineage of Candide, but as a necessary predecessor to Joseph Heller's *Catch-22*, (1955), which is set in Italy at the same time – roughly June

to late September 1944, which has an anti-hero, Yossarian, who is as
afraid as Angelo, and which carries some of Angelo's inspirations a
great deal further. The inspired capitalist Milo Minderbinder, who in
the end takes commissions to bomb his own airfield, seems the heir
of Sergeant Vespucci, the 'Free Distributor' of *Private Angelo*. The
Count said of Vespucci, complacently:

> What a scoundrel the man is, and yet how much we could
> learn from him! For your true rascal is today your only true
> citizen of the world. He plunders all nations without pride
> in one or prejudice against another. He despises frontiers –
> and what an unmitigated nuisance a frontier is! We should
> all learn to hold them in contempt. In bygone times any
> educated man was free to live or travel where he chose,
> but now it is only your rascals who claim such a privilege;
> and there is nothing international in the world but villainy.
> Sergeant Vespucci, who certainly deserves to be shot,
> might serve a better purpose if he were given the chair of
> philosophy in one of our universities. (pp 224-5)

Yossarian and Angelo are both scared, sexy, paranoid and justified.
Yossarian knew people were trying to murder him: 'Yossarian had
proof, because strangers he didn't know shot at him every time he
flew up into the air to drop bombs on them, and it wasn't funny at
all.' (p 19) He concludes, 'The enemy is anybody who's going to get
you killed, no matter *which* side he's on, and that includes Colonel
Cathcart.' (p 143), and it is the old woman left alone in Rome who
concludes: 'Catch-22 says they have a right to do anything we can't
stop them from doing.' (p 467)

Linklater's novel is more temperate than Heller's; it is tempered by
the coming end of hostilities, and the author's love of Italy, which has
no parallel in Heller. Back to *Fanfare* for a last word:

> The subject of my novel was not only war and its capacity
> for destruction, but Italy and its genius for survival. War
> in Italy had a character all its own: it was tragical, as war

inevitably is, but also ludicrous because its waste and folly were underlined, emphasised and thrown into toppling-high relief by the accumulated riches and beauty that Italy had created in the twenty-five centuries since an Etruscan crossed the Tiber and got a she-wolf with twins. War was hateful – anyone could see and say that - but war in Italy was also irrelevant because the forces of civilisation, and the benignities of art, were clearly so much stronger, more informative and more permanent. War, in Italy, was a drunken, destructive and impertinent clown; to deal justly and truthfully with it one had to keep one's temper cool, one's judgment clear, and write a comedy. (F p 316)

NOTES

1. *Fanfare for A Tin Hat*, 1970, p 67. Further references will be given in the text as (F p 000).

2. Cf. pp 114-5.

3. *Among You Taking Notes: The Wartime Diary of Naomi Mitchison,* ed, Dorothy Sheridan, London 1983, p 287; Fussell, p 125.

NAOMI MITCHISON
and *The Bull Calves*

Dates: 1897–1999

Youth and pre-War: Born Edinburgh; raised Oxford. Young lady, studying.

WWI: In London 1915, nursing as a Voluntary Aid Detachment (VAD). Married Dick Mitchison 1916: allowed to nurse Dick in France. First baby 1918.

WW2: Civilian: Ran estate at Carradale; farming, fishing, local politics, Mass Observation diary.

Novels: *Warnings: We Have Been Warned*, 1935; *The Fourth Pig*, 1936; *The Blood of the Martyrs*, 1939; *The Bull Calves*, 1947.

War-related: One-million-word diary for Mass Observation: not intended for publication, but edited by Dorothy Sheridan in 1985 as *Among You Taking Notes: The Wartime Diary of Naomi Mitchison 1939–45*. Memoirs: *All Change Here*, 1975; *You May Well Ask: A Memoir 1920–40*, 1979. Pamphlets on Scottish post-war policies.

Post-War: Local left-wing politician; member of Highland Panel; wife; mother; novelist; children's books; Mother of African Tribe; science fiction; history.

NAOMI MITCHISON was raised in Oxford by Scottish parents. She was profoundly and directly affected by war. She was basically a civilian in both wars, apart from a short but shocking experience treating the wounded as a VAD in a London hospital, but her experience of World War One left a permanent impression in her writing, and in her life. She was sixteen when war broke out, living a very conventionally regulated and privileged home life in Oxford, adoring her big brother Jack and his student friends. She abandoned her science studies at St Anne's and went into nursing, passing exams in 1915 which took her to London, despite family reservations. Her short but grim experience among the wounded made a lasting effect – 'real wounds and real, stinking gangrene' – only ending abruptly when she contracted scarlet fever through milk from an infected farm and was returned home. Jack and his student friends had all joined up from the start, and Jack was performing heroically in the trenches. Even her scientist father was called in to develop a gas mask that worked against German gas attacks. Jenni Calder gives an idea of the ensuing carnage: 'In the four years of war, half a million men under the age of thirty would be killed, including a quarter of the students at Oxford and Cambridge'. [1] Many of the young woman's friends were killed. Soon she became engaged to one of her brother's friends, Dick Mitchison. They married in 1916, and after a week's leave Dick returned to France. There he was severely wounded, with head injury and burns. Naomi went to France with his father to tend him, and with her VAD experience was allowed to nurse him through delirium and suspected brain injury. Before the end of the war, his younger brother and his closest friend were killed.

Small wonder, then, that her first writing was concerned with violence and war, as she struggled to come to terms with the brutality of the facts. She herself said that her experiences came out in her early stories: 'Becoming acquainted with all that pain did something so drastic that I had to write about it, to externalise it on to paper, in order to get it out of my mind: hence the blood and pain in *The Conquered* and my earlier stories'. [2] And she did it well: I recently came across an anthology of the 'best ever' kind, called *The Best War Stories*, published in New York in 1990, which opened with

Mitchison's story 'Black Sparta', first published in 1928. Wars and fighting dominate her early writings about Caesar's Gaul and ancient Greece or Rome. But there was also a more significant and lasting effect, of which Naomi herself only gradually became aware: it meant a huge gulf fixed between her parents' generation and her own. She articulated this in a letter to 'Aunt Bay' in about 1928, which I have already quoted in the Introduction, but which is certainly central enough to quote again:

> I don't believe you realise how much the war has upset our generation – mine and the one immediately after it. ...
> The first wave of disturbance was the one at the time and now we're in for the second, after the period of calm and exhaustion immediately following the thing.... You have still a balance in your life: all that incredible pre-war period when things seemed in the main settled, just moving solidly and calmly like a glacier towards all sorts of progress. But we have had the bottom of things knocked out completely, we have been sent reeling into chaos and it seems to us that none of your standards are either fixed or necessarily good because in the end they resulted in the smash-up. We have to try and make a world for ourselves, basing it as far as possible on love and awareness, mental and bodily, because it seems to us that all the repressions and formulae, all the cutting off of part of our experience, which perhaps looked sensible and even right in those calm years, have not worked. Much has been taken from us, but we will stick like fury to what is left, and lay hold on life, as it comes to us. [3]

The spirit and determination of that last sentence mark all her successive work.

Although she raised several children and had an open marriage, and a wealth of interests, as far as writing went much of the next two decades was taken up with wrestling with the old certainties of behaviour, convention and belief, and questioning the newly proffered answers, trying to formulate new positions which might avert an all-too-possible next war. Mitchison's fiction stopped being set in the ancient world, with whatever covert reference to the present, and began to try to deal with the contemporary. She examined Communism, but found it in the end questionable – 'A lot of Sparta about this', she wrote at the end of her first visit to the Russia on which she had hoped to pin hopes. She and Dick became Labour party members, and he unsuccessfully stood for Parliament twice. She feared the signs in Europe – Fascism in Italy in 1929, Hitler coming to power in Germany in 1933, the civil war in Austria when socialists were crushed by a right-wing opposition in 1934, the outbreak of the Civil War in Spain in 1936. She had sons growing up to provide gun fodder for a next war....

Mitchison conducted her explorations of politics, morality, religion, in public, and formulated warnings to her public in a series of books from 1934. Here are just some, with summary description:

1934　　*Vienna Diary*: a personal account of her visit to 'Red Vienna' during the purge of the socialists – a journey from which she records returning with secret papers stuffed into her knickers.

1935　　*We Have Been Warned*: her first contemporary novel, directly based on her own experiences in Russia and among the English working class, which was withheld from publication for almost two years because the publishers objected to her treatment of rape, and of 'rubber goods'. Not a successful novel, in the end, but a fascinating source. Eventually it was published with cuts, to her lasting annoyance.

1936　　*The Fourth Pig: Stories and Verses*: a series of modern renderings of fairy tales, emphasising the need for fear of dark forces – in the pig's case, the newly greatly magnified wolf – and the danger of piling up riches, and the nature of freedom.

1938   *The Moral Basis of Politics*: a book-length essay spelling out her thinking in layperson's terms rather than philosophic ones. Here she is openly attacking totalitarianism, describing the combination of Nazi mythology, blind obedience and cruelty, and half-suggesting that it was still unclear what side the United Kingdom would take in a (surely) future war.

1939   *The Blood of the Martyrs:* an urgent novel about the persecution of early Christians in ancient Rome, drawing clear parallels with the Nazi persecution of the Jews. The blurb to the Canongate Classics edition reads: 'the novel contains many symbolic parallels to the rise of European fascism in the 1930s and the desperate plight of persecuted minorities such as the Jews and the left-wing activists with whom Naomi Mitchison personally campaigned at the time'.

1939   *The Kingdom of Heaven:* a book in an 'I believe' series, the argument of which describes the series as by writers, by no means all believers, 'opposed to the forces in life which seek to destroy the dignity of the individual human soul and to exalt the machine: who are opposed to the attempt to exalt violence above justice; and to the attempt to substitute persecution for argument'. Here Mitchison endorses the community and social aspects of Christianity.

This list of course does not begin to cover her writing in these years, only those books directly or indirectly concerned with politics, Fascism and the coming of war: it omits a book on Socrates, a history of the home, a modernist fairy tale, poems and plays, and a wealth of articles and reviews. Then comes the biggest gap in Mitchison's phenomenal publishing career: apart from wartime pamphlets and chapters on aspects of post-war reconstruction, her next publication was *The Bull Calves*, in 1947.

So, is there anything in this list that could be singled out as Mitchison's novel of the Second World War? Only if you stretch a lot of points. *We Have Been Warned* (1935) covers a great deal of Mitchison's own experience, discovering working-class life and Labour electorates, and visiting Russia in both hope and fear, and it ends with a fearful vision of Fascist revolution and triumph in England, but it was intended, as its title suggests, as a warning, and it was a warning of what she feared might happen in Britain internally, rather than warning of a future European or world war. *The Blood of the Martyrs* (1939) is more urgently a warning about Germany in particular, and an urging to action of civilised peoples who are trying – probably for the sake of peace – to ignore Nazi persecutions of the Jews and any other nominated enemies of the state. It is a big historical novel about Neronian Rome, of all periods terrifying and unpredictable to humbled and brutalised slaves. The message of Christ reaches some of these most abused of people, and the encouragement of the tiny Christian community brings self-respect and dignity back to some of the most downtrodden.

The method employed here goes back to Mitchison's first novel, *The Conquered* (1923). While rigorously researched and written with clear focus, this novel about Caesar's conquest of Gaul and the divided loyalties of Gallic tribes also succeeded in referring, openly and fairly strongly, to the contemporary situation in Ireland: a glance at the verse epigraphs to each chapter is enough to make this clear. Yeats is quoted thrice, including the well known:

> There's nothing but our own red blood
> Can make a right Rose Tree.

Other verse includes 'The Shan Van Vocht', 'The Croppy Boy' and 'The Bells of Hell go ting-a-ling-a-ling...'

In the case of *The Blood of the Martyrs*, the parallel of Nero with Hitler does not need much seeking out:

> And if the authorities round up a few hundred Christians,
> put them through a solemn trial and find them guilty, then
> they'll get all the curses, and Nero will only have to appear

on his balcony in uniform to have all Rome lining up below
and shouting Hail! (p 232)

Again, Tigellinus encourages Nero with the coming killing of
Christians at the next Games:

> 'All Rome's going to be crazy over you for that,' he added.
> 'They ought to be,' said Nero, 'they ought! When I consider
> what I do for them. Things that none of the others ever
> thought of doing. The music. The spectacles. Strength
> through joy! They ought to be crazy about me. To love me.
>   They ought to do more than love me!' (p 307)

('Strength through joy', of course, as at least some contemporary
readers must have been aware, was the name of the Nazi leisure
and tourism agency.) Nero sees himself as a god, and dreams about
himself and Poppaea: 'Some day they would have a son – a wonder-
child'. (p 310) A much more successful novel than *We Have Been
Warned*, this one still does not deal with the war itself.

Of course, during the war itself Mitchison kept a voluminous
diary for Mass Observation: it is estimated that the manuscript
runs to over a million words. It was not intended for publication,
but Dorothy Sheridan's edited version of 1985 now makes a crucial
contribution to our understanding of the period: *Among You Taking
Notes: The Wartime Diary of Naomi Mitchison 1939-45*.

But here I myself intend to cheat. At the risk of hopelessly
distorting an extremely rich and complex novel, I want to stretch a lot
of points and single out *The Bull Calves* (1947) as Mitchison's most
important fiction concerning the Second World War, despite its being
a historical novel concerning Mitchison's own ancestors shortly after
the Jacobite Rising of 1745. In both historical situations, the war just
done with is the second of the century, for similar causes. In 1986 I
wrote:

> In a wider sense, it draws parallels between the Scottish
> political situation of 1746 and the world situation two

hundred years later, with the culmination of a disastrous
war, and people being called on to clear up the mess. [5]

Douglas Gifford has written so far the best all-round account of the
novel in all its richness, in 'Forgiving the Past: Naomi Mitchison's
The Bull Calves'. He includes agreement with my general point, 'the
responsive reader will not miss the many correspondences between
1747 and 1947… including the fact that major wars have just finished
in the period of the novel and in the author's time.' [6] The rest of this
piece is highly recommended. Gill Plain too recognises the richness
of the novel, describing it as 'a multi-faceted creation: historical
novel, war novel, coming-of-age drama, romance, mystery and
feminist utopia'. [7] She takes on fully, as any serious reader must do,
the fact that the poem with which the novel opens begins with the
death of the writer's infant daughter, Clemency Ealasaid. This, her
seventh child, was intended as her last, the sealing of a permanent
bond between herself and her home in Carradale, Kintyre, where she
was to base herself, becoming increasingly Scottish, for the rest of
her life. Plain sees the book as:

> A fiction of reconstruction; a dream of continuity,
> reconciliation and above all understanding which would
> enable her to escape from the present into a time beyond the
> war, when once again it would be safe to forgive (but not
> forget), to plan and to rebuild. (P p 144)

Plain sees 'baby and book as a bulwark against war', and thinks
that the birth and flourishing of the heroine's own baby, like the
writer's, born late, is significant: 'the health of this child symbolises
a regeneration, the same regeneration that Mitchison desires in a
postwar world.' (P p 160)

So I intend to cheat openly, to follow this thread through the novel,
in the process inevitably doing violence to a more balanced reading,
such as Gifford's, mentioned above. Mine will be piecemeal, marking
some of Mitchison's sporadic returns to the theme.

Even in its form, *The Bull Calves* is an unusual novel, the product in part of an unusual amount of time to ponder. It begins with a poem; it continues with an extended family tree showing the writer's actual descent from the historical characters in the book; it has original, writer-directed illustrations, and after the novel proper it contains a wealth of packed, varied, historical, linguistic and personal notes, in themselves as long as a standard novel. While I would insist that a balanced analysis or survey look at all these, for my purposes I shall ignore the family tree, the illustrations, large sections of the novel, and the notes. The clearest and least ambiguous expression of intent as to a contemporary context as well as an eighteenth-century one is the opening poem.

I'll start with this. 'Clemency Ealasaid', is subtitled 'July 1940', the month Mitchison lost her baby, and the month of a low point in the war when Germany had overrun much of Europe. The up-to-the-minute poem opens with the mother's grief for her dead child, but she soon merges this theme with the chaos of an occupied Europe:

Roll up the map of Europe

Should we try to make sense of a senseless situation?
Over-simplifying, after the habit of the orthodox,
Catholic or Marxist. Shall we try to make sense of Oran?
Try to make sense of inevitable hatred
From mothers of French sailors, babies who had lived
Through the years of hope and pride and delight, boyhood
　　and manhood,
Now murdered by the Ally, perfide Albion?
How make a bargain on that? Roll up the map of Europe.
The lights have gone out: the concentration camps are full:
　　the men and women
Who thought themselves safe have been betrayed to the
　　vultures,
To Himmler, Goering, Franco, to those whose faces
Express Satanic possession. Paris is dead.
Only the bones remain. Paris of the Commune
Dead as the sailors at Oran. This winter we hope to starve

France, Belgium, Holland, Denmark, Norway, Poland:
Harvest of dead babies, disease, hatred: no sense.
My breasts tingle and stab with milk that no one wants,
Surplus as American wheat, surplus and senseless.
Not her soft kind mouth groping for me. Useless, senseless.
If my baby had been starved by England, would I ever
     forgive?
Roll up the map of Europe.

It is characteristic of Mitchison's constant desire to challenge her
reader that she begins this section with an outrage perpetrated by the
British on the French, rather than a German atrocity. Dunkirk and the
fall of Paris happened in June. Early that July, Britain acted to prevent
the French fleet falling into German hands. When the French refused
British offers at Oran, a five minute bombardment left more than 1250
of the French, Britain's recent allies, dead. The poet goes on to lament
the German atrocities, echoing the famous World War One lament,
'The lights are going out all over Europe'. Then she involves British
responsibility again with the new paradox: 'This winter we hope to
starve/ France, Belgium, Holland, Denmark, Norway, Poland'. This
is the logic/illogic of war. She wrote in her Mass Observation diary
that Christmas: 'who are we bombing this Christmas Eve, Christmas
Eve…?' Always the grieving mother shows a maternal female response
to the horrors of war, over-riding nationality: 'If my baby had been
starved by England, would I ever forgive?'

Is Europe like the poet, perhaps too old for 'another birth'? The
poem offers no early answers:

In a hundred years
The French sailors at Oran, the Scottish dead at Abbeville,
The tortured in the concentration camps and all the leaders,
The ones who thought themselves godlike, forgetting the
     Boyg,
And I, and my children, and all the people of Carradale,
We shall be dead, at last out of the running of events and
     hours.

Only then, suggests the poem, can dispassionate forgiveness be offered. But meantime, one sign of hope in the last part of the poem, as throughout the novel, is the planting of trees. Trees planted for Clemency Ealasaid will grow and prosper, as did the trees planted in the novel by the dedicated landowners who turned away from the Prince in 1745 to cultivate Scotland's future in the land. The poem ends by foreseeing a distant future:

> The hot tears will be cooled and the despair of the
>   middle-aged, rolling up their map,
> Will be forgotten, with other evil things, will be interpreted,
> Will be forgiven at last. [8]

The novel will be about the reconciliation and reconstruction of a Scotland divided into warring factions, Highlands and Lowlands, Whig and Tory, with always in the background the canvas painted here, with Scotland almost too small to count in the larger picture. Who can doubt, reading this poem, Mitchison's will to address the European present as well as the Scottish past and present? Of course, inside the text of the novel we will not find direct contemporary reference, but much about the healing of Scottish divisions, which in the light of the preceding poem becomes an image of the larger contemporary European concern.

The novel is in four parts, with interesting titles that suggest first superficial calm and order, then trouble and dark deeds, and finally welcome and warmth. Part One is 'The Smooth Mid-Century'. This can only be ironic, when the subject matter is a Scotland reeling from the divisions newly sharpened by the Forty-Five. The Haldanes of Gleneagles, the bull calves of the title, are Lowlanders who live almost on the Highland Line, and they are officially law-abiding Whigs and Presbyterians who stood back from the Rising. They are having a visit from their sister Kirstie, fairly recently married to Black William, an Episcopalian Highlander who was 'out' in the Fifteen with his father and brother, but who stayed at home occupied with agricultural improvements rather than follow the Prince in 1745. The surface may be smooth and friendly, but much distrust and explanation will be needed before Black William is fully accepted at Gleneagles. This part deals with the new togetherness, but gradually we are also made aware of past feuds still unresolved. One involves Kirstie's favourite brother Patrick, and an old falling out with Duncan Forbes of Culloden, now Lord President. The two are, on the surface, brother Whigs and holding high offices in Scotland. Another much darker one is between Black William and his distant kinsman Kyllachy: here are secrets, inhumane betrayals and enmity, including William's belief that Kyllachy twice betrayed his father to the English government. The whole book is essentially about people or parties on different sides coming to terms with the truth about the past and people's motives, and re-establishing relationships on a sounder basis in peace. Forbes and Patrick will come grudgingly to mutual respect, if not liking, the Haldanes will be united and fully accept William as a brother. Kyllachy is a monstrous character who delights in wounding, and could be said to represent the evils of modern Europe. He will be ignored and isolated – although at one point Patrick suggests rat poison!

The story emerges against a background of Kirstie relating her past to her niece Catherine. A telling moment occurs when Kirstie tells of her father stopping a passionate family dispute over politics: 'There is no set of ideas in the world that is worth a civil war, and between us all we have done enough harm to Scotland!' (p 62) The first part of Chapter Four (pp 70–77) could serve as a lesson or pattern to the parties after World War Two, with a conversation between William and his new brothers-in-law, how they all feel now about the Fifteen and the Forty-Five. Amid the usual positive references to trees we find that sorting out and improving their land is more important now to all than going out to follow a cause: even Black William, who was tempted 'out' after the Prince, says: 'But it was too late…. Our country had begun to save herself other ways. We had seen beyond the Stuarts.' (p 73)

The title of Part Two, 'Ye Highlands ands ye Lowlands', quotes from an old ballad which begins:

Ye Highlands and ye Lowlands
  O whaur hae ye been?
They hae slain the Earl o Murray
  And laid him on the green.

Both Highlands and Lowlands are implicitly blamed for allowing an unnamed 'they' to kill the Earl, a pattern of manly grace. The deed is past: all there is to do now is celebrate the dead. But Part Two actually continues to expose past enmities and present grudges: this culminates in the unexpected arrival of William's distant cousin Kyllachy, the object of his bitter hatred. In this part too the feckless young Jacobite Robert Strange arrives looking for refuge, and both have somehow to be accommodated, however unwillingly.

Kyllachy's efforts to oppose all hopes of peace and reconciliation reach a new depth in Part Three, 'Ill Fishing in Drumlie [troubled, muddy] Waters', as he attempts to hurt in particular William and Kirstie, and Kirstie's beloved but cranky and unreadable brother Patrick. In Chapter Five Patrick, who is both brilliant and insecure and has developed a rather anachronistic sympathy with the common folk of Scotland, reiterates his hatred for Duncan Forbes of Culloden: 'I will keep my own opinions on him.... For I am not changing.' (p 300) This Part ends with the imminent arrival of the ailing Lord President, Duncan Forbes of Culloden, whose tasking job it was to obey or mitigate the vengeful orders of the Duke of Cumberland, victor of Culloden. Forbes and Patrick have been opposed for decades, but a way has to be found to make peace between them when Kyllachy tries to destroy the household: at such a time, men of good will must bury their differences. Almost everyone in the family seems to have put humanity above principle at some point: Kirstie and Black William sheltered a Jacobite female relative and her family; Patrick aided both Black William and his father; Mungo, head of the family, decides not to act when he learns of the Jacobite under his roof – even Forbes, we learn, was kind to William's father when he was in prison. But Captain John, from the East India Company, proves adamant when he learns about Robert Strange in the attic – Kirstie calls it 'a fit of the principles'. Patrick's daughter Margaret speaks up for people over principles: 'You are all half traitors to one thing or another and I have no interest in your politics, but I am standing by my father and Aunt Kirstie!' (p 309)

The wrangling over humane attitudes continues in Chapter Six, leading up to this exchange:

> Captain John said: 'It was unfortunate that your father was a rebel, Borlum. You will admit that it is necessary to root out rebellion.'
> 'By twenty years of prison for an old man that but wanted to stay quiet at home and try out new crops and ways of improvement for Scotland? By dragging out of hiding a young fool that was in the thing by no principle of his own? By ruining a kinsman that has no wish at all to be in the politics and was only there to start with through the over punishment of his father the last time? Think again of your principles, Captain John!' (p 317)

This can surely be a message of a humane kind to a world that will have to come to terms not only with the monsters of Nazidom, but with all manner of others caught up in world events.

Meanwhile, a meeting of minds between Patrick and Forbes looks unlikely: William is afraid of Patrick's likely reaction to Forbes' arrival:

> 'He is a humane and reasonable man and he wants the best for poor Scotland. But he is ill, and a sick man is easy tired and mayna have the will to stand for humanity here – if it is that way he sees it, even. And God knows what your Bear will say to him.' (p 334)

Part Four is entitled 'The Kindly House'. This unusual locution seems to include the suggestion that as well as the house or its inhabitants being 'kindly' disposed to each other and in general, it is their native and congenial rightful home. Here Forbes is apprised of the truth of all the stories. We see his internal struggle:

> And it was too true that there were even yet more than a handful of Jacobite agents in Scotland, the beginnings of trouble that must be stamped out now. Or there would be more follies. And Cumberland again. And hell for Scots folk once more when he himself was in his grave, powerless to stop it. (p 372)

He says that the feckless Jacobite rebel must be arrested, but Strange is found to have escaped. After this he has to continue his hearing from his bed. He listens to all sides, and faces up to Captain John on the matter of principle:

> 'I have maybe another fashion of principle ... and it is not, as you might suppose, merely the expediency of an old man, although that may have something to say in it. But at least I am of age to be judged by my actions, which have ae been those of an honest Whig. Yet I would say that the fountainhead of my principles had been the good of my poor country, Scotland, which has been so sore torn by the politics. I knew fine that nothing but harm could come to us from the Stewarts, for all we have had so little good of the house of Hanover. But after the troubles were past – gentlemen, you will likely mind of how I counselled mercy to Cumberland and the rest after the battle.' (p 388)

He goes on with his general 'message':

> I ... had the opinion that this was the correct moment for both mercy and compromise. These are not virtues at easy times when they come naturally to all of us. But only at difficult times such as the present.' (pp 388-9)

Finally he offers an olive branch to Patrick, which is accepted: both have the good of the Scottish people in the forefront of their thoughts. And he offers a final aspiration to those in the room and contemporary Europe:

> We in Scotland have been over much battered to be able to spare any man who will set his hand and mind to the future. Aye, or any woman, Kirstie! We must act together and build ourselves up slowly and surely, by way of the peaceful arts and trades through commerce and agriculture, until we are well of our wounds. ... Aye, Scotland will need all of us. And in a while things will begin to go as they should. (p 389)

This summary has shown massive disrespect to the novel, by ignoring the personal accounts and confessions of Kirstie and William in particular, which are usually seen as central to the novel, but it may be enough to support my case that, as well as whatever else it is, *The Bull Calves* is concerned with the potential aftermath of the Second World War.

AFTERWORD

Mitchison wrote only one children's book which dealt directly with the war, *The Rib of the Green Umbrella* (1960). She recalls the conception of this book in a late memoir, *Mucking Around: Five Continents over Fifty Years* (1981):

> I expect I let go to places, encouraging them to sink in and start a fertilisation process which might end in a story or poem. ... Yet perhaps it came at me most strongly in San Gimignano, not that I am the only writer to be gripped by that background. (p 16)

I suspect one writer she had in mind here was her friend Eric Linklater, and the novel *Private Angelo*. This story has a lot of Italian village background in common with *Private Angelo*, and a similar theme, the attempt to preserve masterpieces of Italian art from the depradations of war. While it is true, for example, that there are three versions of Uccello's *Battle of San Romano*, it is quite a coincidence, to say the least, that this is one picture that is among the array of treasures Linklater found stored in the country during the fighting, and it is also to be found among the treasures of the small museum run by Piero's grandfather:

> There was another painting of a pink horse and a pale blue horse rearing, and the men riding them had great spears, too big to be real. ... Yet he couldn't stop looking at these horses that had been painted by Paolo Uccello such a long time ago. (pp 18-9)

I think I detect a playful, private 'writer's wink' to her predecessor here. Mitchison and Linklater had flown together to an international PEN Conference in Zurich in May 1947, when the success of *Private Angelo* was at its height. Both books certainly concern the Italian Resistance, and self-proclaimed German lovers of Italy and Italian art. And where Angelo ends his novel, 'We have learnt the most useful of all accomplishments, which is to survive!' (p 272), here the German Hauptmann says bitterly to Piero's Italian grandfather, 'You, of course, will survive.' (p 123) In *Private Angelo* the art-loving German Schlemmer shoots up the Piero della Francesca *Adoration of the Shepherds*, while in *Rib of a Green Umbrella* the Hauptmann takes all the grandfather's dearest treasures after he learns of the death of his own wife. But it is characteristic of Mitchison that she is mindful of her child readership: more than once we have comments like that of Piero's mother: 'He did it out of dreadful unhappiness. Perhaps we ought not to judge him. It is the war.' (p 125) And it is appropriate to the madness of war that we learn that the Hauptmann's wife, home and city have been destroyed by Allied attack – and that his home city was Dresden.

> Wars make people like that, Papa. Later on perhaps many will have regrets. On both sides it may be. (p 142)

NOTES

1   Jenni Calder, *The Nine Lives of Naomi Mitchison*, 1997, Virago, p 39.

2   *All Change Here: Girlhood and Marriage*, 1975, Bodley Head, pp 127–8.

3   Quoted in Jill Benton, *Naomi Mitchison: A Biography*, 1990, Pandora, p 50.

4   *The Kingdom of Heaven*, 1940, p viii.

5   See Isobel Murray, ed, *Beyond this Limit: Selected Shorter Fiction of Naomi Mitchison*, 1986, Edinburgh, Introduction p xv.

6   See *Studies in Scottish Fiction: Twentieth Century*, eds, Joachim Schwend and Horst W Drescher, 1990, Frankfurt, p 222.

7   See *Women's Fiction of the Second World War: Gender, Power and Resistance*, 1966, Edinburgh University Press, p 142. Further references will be given in the text as (P p 000).

8   'Clemency Ealasaid' has also been printed separately in *Shadows of War: British Women's Poetry of the Second World War,* ed, Anne Powell, pp 62-5. I have dealt with this poem in more detail in 'Clemency Ealasaid: July 1940: The Turning Point in a Poet's War' in *Scottish Studies Review* Volume 6, No 2, Autumn 2005, pp 72–83.

FRED URQUHART
and what led to *Jezebel's Dust*

Dates: 1912–1995.

Youth and Pre-War: Born Edinburgh. Peripatetic childhood following father's job – Berwickshire, Fife, Perthshire, Wigtownshire, Edinburgh. Bookseller.

WW2: Conscientious objector. Tribunals sent him to farming work near Laurencekirk in North East Scotland.

Novels: *The Ferret Was Abraham's Daughter*, 1949; *Jezebel's Dust*, 1951.

Post-War: Writer, with occasional jobs in the book trade: short-story-writer and novelist, London and Sussex.

FRED URQUHART was very definitely Scottish: he told me when he was eighty that he still thought in Scots, although he had lived for decades in the South of England. But somehow he has escaped the consciousness of most of those concerned with Scottish literature. This could be in part because he doesn't belong to 'his own' area of Scotland, as Grassic Gibbon to the North East, or Robin Jenkins to Glasgow and Argyll. One obvious reason for this is that his childhood was peripatetic: the family followed the father round a series of chauffeuring posts, Edinburgh, Granton. Perthshire, Wigtownshire. The boy attended three primary schools, and two senior, at the last of which he was unhappy. This was Broughton in Edinburgh, and Urquhart left aged fifteen, obviously not qualified for university, and spent seven years working in an Edinburgh bookshop, years which were to be vital to the material of his future writing.

Urquhart was not a 'joiner' on the Scottish literary scene, and eventually found company more to his liking in and around London's Soho, where he mingled with artists and writers in a lively gay scene. His sexual preference always stood somewhat in the way of his living in Scotland and writing about Scottish people, where prejudice about sexual mores was strong. Ironically, this is probably what led to his growing reputation in the thirties as a short story writer who was particularly good at drawing women. Stevie Smith declared, 'He does women very well', and John Pudney said Urquhart's specialities were 'good dialogue and bad women'. Especially in view of the books I mean to concentrate on here, I suggest that he was right about the dialogue, but too narrow about the women. In his stories Urquhart creates girls of all sorts, girls with shattered dreams or cruel boyfriends, women coarse or fine, comic or pathetic or downright unattractive – one is hefty, with a wall eye, dung-splashed legs, and fingers 'like rationed red sausages'.

The first Scottish scene Urquhart knew well as an adult outside Edinburgh was the result of another 'oddity'. He was a (non-religious) conscientious objector. Eventually he was granted exemption from serving in the Second World War if he would go into agricultural work. In 1940, he wrote about his first tribunal for the public in 'Let us endure an Hour: A Conscientious Objector in England'. [1] He was refused credence, and it was only after an appeal tribunal that he was sent to the farm. He came to a farm near Laurencekirk, a move which would result in a great flowering of short stories, which have been compared with those of Grassic Gibbon and Jessie Kesson. If readers associate Urquhart with any part of Scotland, then, it is likely to be the Mearns. But after the war he soon hightailed it back to London and the South, working in different aspects of the book trade, and living a fairly isolated life in Sussex with his partner, Peter Wyndham Allen, whom he celebrated in "Forty-Three Years: A Benediction", his account of 'a happy homosexual marriage'. [2]

All these factors and no doubt more contributed to Urquhart's remaining a solitary Scottish voice, rarely heard in literary debate. It was exacerbated by the reaction to his conscientious objection. He suffered unknown, untold obloquy during and after the war. His public persona affected not to care what anyone thought, but he clearly remained privately very nervous of other people's potential reaction. As late as 1989 he wrote to the publisher of *Full Score*, an edition of his best stories, asking him to remove a reference from the Introduction:

> I see no necessity for any reference to my own conscientious objection. My anti-war views are clearly expressed in many of the stories. I've lived in this corner of South East England for thirty years, and all my friends are either dead or have gone to other parts. Almost all my acquaintances now are flag-waving reactionaries, so I don't want…. to raise again the acrimony I suffered in the war years. [3]

Urquhart's first published novel, *Time Will Knit*, came out in 1938. While keeping to its historical setting, the time of the First World War, Urquhart exploits obvious parallels with the years leading up to the Second. It is clear that this is another warning against war. Here is a typical working-class family, where the father's socialist and pacifist beliefs are upheld by the sons, and yet of course they are helpless to resist war. One son shares the father's beliefs, but still enlists, to get it over with. Another is literally driven mad by swarms of whitefeather-delivering women, and the father despairs because he thinks he has not enough reading to argue his case convincingly. War as a capitalistic enterprise, inimical to the workers, is a dominant theme, part of an even wider argument about the disadvantages suffered by the working-class, in life generally, in education, in career choice. That line will echo through much of Urquhart's fiction: 'I/he/she never had a chance.' It is brilliantly chosen, because in most cases it is factually true, but when uttered by a character it can sound perilously like a whine. It echoes through *The Ferret Was Abraham's Daughter* and *Jezebel's Dust*. The knitting metaphor in *Time Will Knit* refers to the interweaving of narrators whose thoughts we overhear, different members of the family, from old and done to the bright young American cousin Spike. Urquhart said it was an attempt to imitate Virginia Woolf: 'My one desire was to write interior monologues in Scots'. [4] The results are uneven: some characters have difficulty when required by the story to relate significant family events for the reader to 'overhear', but it is a most readable and ambitious first novel.

And it gets its message across, even at the cost of straining credulity. Un-educated the father may be, and under-privileged he certainly is, but he has times of eloquence. Here is part of a set-piece:

> There must have been millions of homes like ours, both in Britain and Germany, where some of the sons were going out to fight because they thought their mothers and sisters and sweethearts were in danger of being assaulted as the lying pro-rich-man-and-his-profits papers said. Millions of homes where the other sons held the view that if everybody refused to fight the war would automatically stop and those who engineered it would need to sue for whatever peace-terms they could get. Millions of homes where young mothers, like Bella, were torn between anxiety for their bairns and undecided whether to force their husbands to go and fight for them at the front or to stay and defend them at home. Millions of homes where young women, like Kate, were being proud and happy because their brothers were soldiers, because it allowed them to crow over their less

fortunate (or more!) friends who had no brothers or fathers in uniform. Millions of husbands like Jim Anderson who didn't want to go and be killed, but who, above all, didn't want their wives and families to perish.... (pp 196–7)

This novel was followed by a spate of stories, some written during the war itself, leaping off the pages of small magazines in their immediacy. A selection of titles illustrates this, and gives some indication of his favourite subject matter: 'Blackout'; 'Mrs Coolie-hoo's Pole'; 'I Fell for a Sailor'; 'Namietnosc – Or The Laundry Girl and the Pole'; 'The Last G.I. Bride Wore Tartan'. Civilian girl or woman meets foreign soldier(s) or sailor(s), and some kind of relationship ensues. Some of these stories were eventually used as drafts for parts of the two novels I want to concentrate on.

The two novels were published separately, *The Ferret Was Abraham's Daughter* in 1949, and *Jezebel's Dust* in 1951. But Urquhart meant them to be read as one. He told Hugh Macpherson in 1992 that they were,

> Really one long story about two Edinburgh 'good-time' girls
> who cavorted around with Poles, Free French, and every
> man they could lay their hands on. One of them became
> a GI Bride, while the other went to gaol for stabbing her
> Polish lover. [5]

The novelist has learned a lot about novel-writing since *Time Will Knit*, and these books are far less obviously 'anti war'. And his choice of focus, on the careers of very young 'good-time girls', is a surprise for a start. Angus Calder writes, 'the first of September 1939 was to have been the day when the school-leaving age would have been raised from fourteen to fifteen.' [6] So narrowly did Bessie Hipkiss, rising fourteen, miss qualifying to be a child evacuee, and start her new career. Urquhart's two connected novels give a vivid picture of life in wartime Edinburgh, and an equally vivid picture of the pressures young girls with few prospects were subjected to.

John Costello has a factual social history of what happened

to young civilian women (or rather girls) which gives a bleak impression of their lives and possible futures, whether in the USA or in Britain. For many, family pressures were lightened or lifted, while entrancing foreign soldiers from many nations filled city streets with smart uniforms, showy manners, glamour, and ready money. Some girls married, like Lily McGillivray, for the allowance paid to soldiers' wives, and some of these, like Lily, as soon forgot their husbands. The 'good-time girl' had a heyday, and a number of predictable outcomes followed. There was a steep rise in illegitimacy, and the number of divorces was set to rise, as the infidelities under the unnatural pressures of war rose too. Costello details the great variety of girls faced with illegitimate – and often unwanted – babies:

> Some were adolescent girls who had drifted away from homes which offered neither guidance nor warmth and security.... There were decent and serious, superficial and flighty, irresponsible and incorrigible girls among them. There were some who had formed serious attachments and hoped to marry. There were others who had a single lapse, often under the influence of drink. There were, too, the 'good-time girls' who thrived on the presence of well-paid servicemen from overseas, and semi-prostitutes with little moral restraint. But for the war many of these girls, whatever their type, would never have had illegitimate children. (pp 276-7) [7]

And at the same time there were still families like John Guthrie's in *Sunset Song* where the father would dictate, whether out of religious principle or pure selfishness, that his wife submit to serial pregnancies, to her physical detriment, or even death.

All these elements are to be found in *The Ferret Was Abraham's Daughter* (1949), but Urquhart's inspired story-telling, his authentic-sounding dialogue, his internal monologues, all conspire to paint a very different and very vivid picture. Given that these books have only just come back into print from Kennedy and Boyd, and that they have been unobtainable, even on the internet, my account will be largely descriptive. They are comic and satiric, although with a basic anger at what the war is making of the young girls, and some pity, at least for Bessie. The titles are the first problem: Urquhart's story titles tend to be punchy, colloquial and memorable, but these two are different. *The Ferret Was Abraham's Daughter* is the early story of Bessie Hipkiss, a young girl in Edinburgh whose mother dies in (unwanted) childbirth, leaving her to bring up the younger children and housekeep for her father, while that patriarch sacrifices Bessie to her family duty. Red-haired Bessie is nicknamed the Ferret. *Jezebel's Dust* is a striking phrase from a dense Donne sermon, about how death levels all.

Bessie Hipkiss is perforce, the 'heroine' of both books, the central consciousness, the Chris Guthrie equivalent, if you like. But realisation dawns on the reader that Bessie is pathetic, shallow, tawdry and pliable. Only one thing marks her out. Like Urquhart himself as a boy, she has a great propensity to daydream. In an autobiographical essay he wrote of his boy-self: 'I was teeming with all kinds of far-fetched dreams from being the lost heir to an Italian dukedom to bowing deeply to the applause in a great theatre in New York'. [8] So he could write with real empathy about poor Bessie's dreams of being the Duchess de Bourbon-Parma, of the lost French royal family. Her dreams are in themselves touchingly tawdry, spun from her reading of Dumas and her inveterate cinema-going. The cinema-going makes her very typical. Angus Calder concludes: 'Probably most people under forty saw at least fifty feature films every year'. Paul Fussell adds: 'in the 1940s the cinema delineated little but a fairy-tale world of uncomplex heroism and romantic love, sustained by toupees, fake bosoms, and happy endings'. [9]

Bessie's school teacher is impressed by her imagination, and encourages her to think of her future with ambition, but the usually inconspicuous narrator importantly comes in early to clarify things for the reader. After this, interpretation will largely be up to the reader, and the novel will unfold in lively dialogue and private emotion. Here is a new and uncomfortable kind of heroine for the Scottish novel:

'Do ye think ye'll like to be a teacher, hen?'

'I dinnie ken,' Bessie muttered.

She had no ideas about what she wanted to be. Her father and Miss Aitchison said she was to be a teacher, so she accepted that uncomplainingly. She was not clever enough to reason it out within herself. If she had been, she would have known that she hadn't enough brains to be a teacher. She had no head for mathematics, geography, science or any of the other subjects, even in their simplest forms. All she was really gifted with was a good imagination, and it was this imagination as shown in her school essays which had made Miss Aitchison insist to Bert Hipkiss that he allow Bessie to stay on at school. If Bessie had been clever enough to be honest with herself she would have known that what she really wanted was to spend her life day-dreaming. But actually she was rather stupid. In many ways she did not have even the low cunning of some of her contemporaries at school or in the neighbourhood. She had a simplicity which verged at times almost on the moronic. Her life was bound up with her mother and the fantasies she wove for herself and the children, especially those she wove for herself. In some vague way she was dissatisfied with her life and environment, but she knew no way of changing it unless by escape into day-dreams. She knew no other life, except the ones she read about in novels or saw on the films. (pp 30-1)

The story is told mainly through dialogue and tuning in to Bessie's thoughts or reactions. It is fascinating in itself, this glimpse of working-class Edinburgh in the year before the war really got started. We follow the introduction of the blackout, the provision of air-raid shelters, the   imposition of gas-masks, the evacuation of young children, and, most importantly for Lily and Bessie in their quest for men, the darkened city streets at night, and their gradual filling up with exotic foreigners, Norwegians, Czechs, Poles, Free French. Lily splutters, 'Honest to God, Ferret, you take the cake! I can see that you and me are goin' to have some fun before this war's lasted much longer', and the war opens up boundless new fields for Lily in particular (p 124). Bessie is rising fourteen at the start of the book, and Lily a mere six months older, but Lily has already become her own idea of a woman: 'Lily, like lots of other people, had a damned fine time in the blackout' (p 164). It is a time of social confusion, melting custom and producing a new 'class' of variously inclined 'good-time girls.'

Bessie's mother is exhausted from child-bearing: she lost her last baby, and is rightly apprehensive about the one she is expecting, sharing her fear with Bessie. In the event, she dies in childbed in March 1939, leaving the family to the fourteen-year-old's ignorant and unwilling mercies. Her father, the Abraham of the title, complacently expects Bessie to sacrifice any future she might have to caring for the two older children and the new baby, and putting his meals on the table immediately on his return from work. The new baby does not thrive, and Bessie cannot like him. He lasts three months, then dies. But not before Bessie has been genuinely tempted to kill him. And it must be admitted that the two older children are neither attractive nor amenable: Billie is by turns a pugnacious street urchin and a lisping babyish boy, and Jenny is a small tyrant, full of demands for stories, efforts to peek at Bessie's breasts, and threats to say a Bad Word, or worse:

> 'I want to be bad,' she yelled. 'I'm goin' to be BAD.' She slipped from her chair. 'I'm goin' to say Bad Words, and I'm goin' to take off my breeks and do a wizzy on the floor. I'm goin' to do a lot of wizzies.' (p 6)

At the very start, then, these are the worlds that clash for Bessie, her royal day-dreams, which can move her to tears, and the crude realities of daily struggles at home:

> She was walking beside the Ambassador from the Court of Spain up the white marble stairs of the Louvre to where her

father, the King of France, was holding a levee. The heralds
were announcing her: 'Her Royal Highness, Madame
Elisabeth, Duchess de Bourbon-Parma, Duchess de Guise,
Duchess d'Orleans... .'
   She opened the door.
   'Is that you, Bessie?' her mother shouted. 'Take Jenny to
the lavvy, will you? She wants to do a wizzy.' (p 3)

The first novel deals with all this, and Bessie's first steps in the world
Lily inhabits, where soldiers are fancied above civilians, and officers
above other ranks, and sailors above all, because Lily has a weakness
for the uniform. And this is a world where Edinburgh streets are
suddenly flooded with uniformed foreigners, all apparently ready to
show girls a good time. Bessie is very childish in some ways: she hates
her surname, Hipkiss, and the coarse jokes schoolmates make about
it, and she abruptly sheds her first real boyfriend when he is called up
and they mean to love and write forever – until she learns his name
is Smellie.

   By August, Bessie's father introduces 'Aunt Mabel', and before
Christmas they are married, and Bessie - and her dead mother - are
displaced. Eventually she leaves home to be a maid of all work for Mrs
Irvine who runs a guesthouse, an imposing matron with a high-flown
line in spiritualism. Meantime, we have participated in air-raids, and
gossip by the Co-op van, slovenly neighbours poking uninvited noses
in, the evacuation of the younger children, tenement life in the raw.
And in front of this backdrop, as it were, the two girls, Lily leading,
Bessie following, prancing in high heels, discovering peroxide, and
becoming blatant blondes. In this book Bessie preserves her virtue,
more by luck than good guidance. Good guidance is something she
sadly lacks. Bessie is hopelessly weak, dependent always on other
people, overwhelmed with bad – or selfish – guidance, from her father,
from Lily, from Mrs Irvine, from neighbours. In the next novel there
will also be a series of men: she is lucky only at the end of *Jezebel's
Dust*, because of the pertinacity, solidity and steadiness of Norman
Gantz, who becomes her rock. From early on, the narrator has warned:
'she needed somebody on whom to fasten her attention.' (p 200)

With the book until now virtually unobtainable, perhaps the easiest way to get a sketchy profile of Bessie is to compare and contrast her with Chris Guthrie, the heroine of Scotland's 'favourite book', *Sunset Song*. I do not know whether the similarities and differences of these young girls are deliberate, but they are striking. Urquhart could be deliberately shadowing his distinguished predecessor for contrast. Gibbon and Urquhart choose adjacent situations. In a short time, when the girl is in her teens, Chris's mother, afraid of another ordeal in childbirth, kills herself. She also kills her twin babies, it has been suggested so as not to burden Chris. Like Bessie's mother, she has already had a stillbirth. Bessie's mother is equally and rightly afraid, and she does die in childbed, with the baby only surviving her for a few weeks. But she has left Bessie to care for Billie and Jenny, and all depends on her sense of love and duty, and the expectations of others. Chris is left to choose for herself between the world of school and education, possibly becoming a teacher, or to go back to work the land: either is easily within her grasp. Bessie never really had any chance of being a teacher, or any strength of mind to make a real decision. Chris is capable of acting – and living – on her own, of accepting bleak realities and surviving alone: Bessie is weak, dependent always on other people, and she only survives because of the benign accident by which, in *Jezebel's Dust*, she meets and marries Norman Gantz. It is striking in both books how much happens, and when the heroine is really very young.

The main figure we compare and contrast with Bessie in *Jezebel's Dust* is, of course, Lily. This was Urquhart's favourite novel, the one he always hoped to see reprinted. The girls are exposed to all the temptations and dangers of civilian life in a wartime city, and Lily gradually but determinedly goes 'to the bad'. Everyone warns Bessie against her, to no avail. By degrees Lily tires of different jobs and begins to steal or shoplift. She marries a sailor early on, but as Mrs Irvine is quick to point out, 'She just did it to get a marriage allowance from the Government.' She forgets Tommy inside two months, and is on the hunt for new men, and cannot find time to read his letters. The new novel opens just after Dunkirk (June 1940), and the city – and Mrs Irvine's boarding house – fills up with foreign soldiers. Lily leads Bessie on determined manhunts, and never seems faithful to any one pick-up, until she is unfortunate enough to meet the Pole Tadeuz Zabanski, with whom she has a troubled relationship, leaving him for a better off Colonel, but eventually going back, despite her knowledge of his violent nature and readiness with a knife. She uses Bessie as a foil whenever it suits her, and neglects her otherwise. She bullies her endlessly, making her drink coffee instead of tea, insisting her unwilling friend visit pubs, calling her a liar when the reverse is the case, until poor Bessie doubts herself. Lily is less involved with the plot in this novel, but notably and perilously betrays Bessie toward the end, giving her address to the predatory Pole Klosowski who is after her with nefarious intent.

In *Jezebel's Dust* the five parts into which the book is divided are more noticeable than in the previous novel. They rather resemble the acts of a play, with each leading up to a fairly climactic scene. Part One begins when Bessie has been six months at Mrs Irvine's and is very excited at the house filling up with a variety of foreign officers. She reacts in particular to the advent of the two Poles, Dmitri Klosowitz and 'Joe Pole' Rolewicz, who click their heels and bow from the waist. Again, Bessie's reaction seems fairly typical. Longmate confirms: 'In most places, especially in Scotland, it was the Poles who came first and, until the Americans arrived, made the greatest impact.'[10] Most of the foreigners in the book are Poles, and some, like Klosowski and Lily's Teddy Gabanski, are both polite and ruthless. But Joe Pole is a good and honest man, who prevents any hostile national generalisations. Bessie is excited by Klosowski and Rolewicz, even before she feels a preference for the tall blonde Joe, who has no English. But it is Klosowitz who begins to haunt her, and instinctively she is 'vaguely afraid' (p 38) of him. He eyes her, says the narrator, 'slyly and smiling with anticipatory greed.'

The disarming straightforwardness of his approach confounds Bessie. She has been to the cinema alone on a night off, and the News Reel deals with the fall of France. She is carried away, and 'for the first time in weeks and weeks', resumes her old dreams of being 'Elizabeth, Duchess de Bourbon-Parma, Madame Royale of France...' She bursts out sobbing,

'Ah, ma belle Paree!' Bessie sobbed, 'Ma belle Paree, ... Vive
la France!'
Tears were streaming down her cheeks, but she made no move
to check them. Waves of icy excitement were sweeping over
her. She stood beside Churchill on a balcony, looking down at
the soldiers and guns and tanks going past.... (p 47)

We are reminded how very young she is, and how close dream and
reality can come for her. Soon after, she is looking at dresses in a
shop window when Klosowski comes up to her and asks which one
she likes best. He says he will get it for her, and will teach her to
ride a horse, and she flounders, at a loss. When an air-raid siren
sounds, he grips her tightly round the waist, and in the darkness of
the shelter he kisses her fiercely. The following day, the dress of her
dreams is delivered, and the charwoman persuades her to try it on:

Bessie would have liked to have opened the box slowly and
to let her imagination linger over the dress as she put it on.
But she had been hustled so quickly into it that still she had
not fully realised what it all meant. (p 65)

Nor does she, until too late. When Mrs Irvine says she must return
it, she is grievously disappointed. But Klosowski's polished manners
triumph again, and he persuades Mrs Irvine to let her keep it. At
bedtime she is thinking more kindly of him and dreaming again of
France when the Pole comes to her room and swiftly and surely takes
his payment for the dress. Bessie does not resist for long, and so ends
Part One.

Part Two begins with Bessie's father joining up as a lorry driver in
the RAOC in September 1940. Inside three weeks Bessie encounters
two old neighbours who announce that her 'steppy' has openly
taken up with a Pole, and that her father ought to know about it.
Meantime, Klosowski has to go on manoeuvres for at least a month,
which causes Bessie very mixed feelings. She enjoys showing him off
to Lily, but is basically relieved he has gone, and manages to put him
out of mind, although she knows he will soon return:

> It was a relief to know that she could go to bed without
> either locking her door or lying awake, listening for quiet
> tiptoeing outside her door and then *that*. Although it had
> happened only twice, Bessie was in no doubt about what it
> all meant. It was wonderful, of course. Far far better than
> she had imagined from any of the books she had read or
> what she had heard. But she knew that it was *wrong*. (p 82)

Even to herself she doesn't quite voice the possibility of pregnancy.
Her fatal lack of reality has her dreaming of a romantic future
with Klosowski in Poland – until three days later, when Joe Pole
asks her out. They start to go steady, and go dancing with Lily
and her Tadeuz, to celebrate the dress Klosowski gave her. Lily and
Tadeuz are now living together, and Tadeuz has already threatened
revenge on an employer of Lily's with a knife, the first mention of
this weapon, but by no means the last. At the dance, Teddy draws
the knife on a Frenchman who offers to dance with Lily. On the
way home, Joe Pole makes *his* move on Bessie in the Meadows. A
pleasant fear is replaced by 'warm, sensual ecstasy' (p 114), and they
sleep together for the next few weeks, Bessie managing to forget
Klosowski's imminent return the while. When he does unexpectedly
return, she is afraid, but at first he keeps his distance. But this is
only to give Bessie a false sense of security. A week later she delivers
towels to his room and finds herself trapped and locked in there, he
in scarlet silk dressing gown and brandishing a riding crop. Now
he will teach her to ride a horse – and he goes down on hands and
knees, commanding her to mount him and use the whip. She has to
pull on riding breeches while he throws off the dressing gown – and
at last she finds her voice and screams the place down. The whole
house assembles to witness the final scene between Klosowski and
Mrs Irvine, and her dismissal of him instantly. But Bessie has had a
terrible fright, and has a lurking fear that he might surface again in
her life at some point.

Part Three is set back at home, where popular opinion has decided
Bessie must return, because her 'steppy' has departed with *her* Pole,
'the man I love', and just deserted the children. Unwillingly she

resumes home duties, although with the consolation of Joe visiting her every night. Lily enters Bessie's life again, if only to announce her imminent departure for London with her new-found colonel, but in the process she drops a bombshell into the tired, dull monotony of Bessie's days. Bessie is so innocent, so ignorant and so unreflective that she has not noticed she is pregnant – either by Klosowski or Joe Pole – and about five months gone! As she leaves, Lily urges her to get Mrs Irvine to sort it out and get her married to Joe. But before the horrified and reluctant Bessie has time to confide in Joe, her father abruptly arrives home to attend to the family crisis, and storms at the pair to leave, forming another dramatic scene.

Before Part Four begins, time passes, and we next encounter Bessie Rolewicz in London in the summer of 1942. She is staying with a friend of Mrs Irvine, and preparing to meet Lily coming out of gaol after doing six weeks for shop-lifting. She had gone back to Teddy, despite his unstable and violent record. Joe meantime is serving in Africa. But there is no baby! We learn in retrospect how Bessie had gone out, heavily pregnant, for a short walk, and panicked at an air-raid warning. She was helped by a tall American GI who led her to the shelter, stayed with her when she fainted, and even accompanied her in the ambulance. This decent American's behaviour is in sharp contrast to that of the predatory Klosowski, who had kissed her so violently in an earlier shelter. The baby lived only a few hours, a matter for sadness but a certain relief – Bessie was by no means ready for the responsibilities of motherhood. The friendly GI, Norman Gantz, remains friendly and respectful, a good friend. A year on, Bessie is finding it hard to remember the absent Joe Pole's face, although she is determined that she loves her husband, and is pleasantly but guiltily haunted by Norman's. Towards the end of Part Four, he has asked her out. Friends urge her to go. She can't decide, and while she swithers comes news that Joe has been wounded, and is unable to write. She turns down Norman's invitation, but is later bullied into going to the cinema with Lily. She comes home to bad news:

> That night when Bessie returned to the boarding house about eleven o'clock she found a telegram to say that

Lieutenant Josef Rolewicz had died of wounds received in battle. (p 174)

In Part Five, events move to a squalid climax. In a third air-raid shelter scene, Bessie and Norman encounter Lily and her latest beau, and Norman is definitely unimpressed: 'I hate to see a dame all plastered with powder like your friend Lily... She's too tough a babe for me... she's rank poison.' (p 193) He proposes they marry in three weeks, after he has completed a course in Devon. For the last time, Bessie is left vulnerable without him. Lily is jealous of his proposal, on financial grounds: 'Lookit you. You're laughin' kit-bags. A widdy's pension and now a Yank wantin' to marry you. Huh, you're in the money all right, Bessie Hipkiss!' (p 201) Lily no longer wants a job, and can do well enough without one:

'Are you not goin' to get another job, Lil?'
    'Och, why should I? I manage all right. Why the hell should I work if I can find mugs o' men that are willin' to pay for me?... Ach, be your age, Ferret. After all I'm no' the only one, not by a long chalk.' (p 205)

The conversation gets personal, with Lily threatening to tell Norman about Bessie's past with the two Poles. Three days before Norman's return, Bessie has an unexpected and unwelcome visitor, Dmitri Klosowski. He got her address from an obliging Lily, and claims Lily is ill and needs her. But she finds Lily's bed empty – and ready. A scene as from a B movie ensues, with Klosowski locking the door and Bessie holding him off with a poker. He too now threatens to tell Norman about their past relationship – unless she is *nice* to him again. As Bessie screams for help, Lily and Teddy arrive to save the situation for the time, while continuing a fight they bring with them. Lily persuades Bessie to have a cuppa before they both leave, and they find the kitchen rank and unpleasant. Tadeuz has called Lily a tart, and a prostitute: now he demands she make coffee for the men, and finally he threatens her in turn: 'You must remember, my dear Lily, there are certain things which I know about you, which would be very unpleasant for you, if I spoke about them'. (pp 219-20) He goes on to detail them, until she threatens him with murder, and he threatens her physically until the knife slips from Lily and appears to land in Gabanski's chest. (This turns out to be a bloody but non-fatal flesh wound.)

The seven-page epilogue takes the form of Bessie, the mother of three children and 'one of Willow Creek's prominent young matrons' (pp 224-5), having to tell stories to her children as she used to do to Billy and Jenny. She tells of the trial and Lily's imprisonment. But perhaps the last word goes to old Mr Powys, bystander:

> 'Poor child,' Mr Powys had said. 'It isn't her we should judge. It's society that's to blame. If they will have wars, they must put up with the troubles that wars bring in their wake, A short life and a gay one! Can we blame the unfortunate girl for wanting to have a good time while she could?' (pp 228-9)

And Bessie reflects, 'In a way it was just sheer luck that she hadn't been standing in that dock instead of Lily. She might have struck Klosowski with the poker'. So Bessie does not prevail because she is the traditionally virtuous heroine: accident and luck have saved her.

NOTES

1   See 'Let Us Endure an Hour: A Conscientious Objector in England', in *The Southern Literary Messenger*, March, 1941, pp 133–7.

2   See *New Writing Scotland* No 11: *The Ghost of Liberace*, eds, A L Kennedy and Hamish Whyte, ASLS, 1993, pp 135-146.

3   I am grateful to J Graeme Roberts, editor of *Full Score*, for access to his papers concerning Urquhart: here, a letter from Urquhart to Colin Maclean at AUP, 2nd February, 1989.

4   See an interview with Urquhart by Alan Bold in *The Scotsman*, 19th July, 1980.

5   See Hugh Macpherson in *The Scottish Book-Collector*, February/March, 1992, pp 27–30.

6   Calder (1969), p 55.

7   John Costello, *Love, Sex and War: Changing Values 1939–45*, 1985, p 276–7.

8   See 'My Many Splendoured Pavilion' in *As I Remember: Ten Scottish Authors Recall how Writing Began for them*, ed, Maurice Lindsay, 1979, pp 157–174.

9   Calder (1969), 424: Fussell, p 189.

10 Norman Longmate, *How We Lived Then: A History of Everyday Life During the Second World War*, London, 1971, p 188.

ROBIN JENKINS
and *Guests of War*

Dates: 1912–2005.

Youth and Pre-War: Born Flemington; Hamilton Academy; Glasgow University, English; Teacher training; teaching in Glasgow.

WW2: Escorted evacuation of Glasgow children to Moffat; Conscientious objector: two tribunals: sent to forestry in Argyll, 1940–46.

Novels: *Guests of War*, 1956; *Fergus Lamont*, 1979; *Just Duffy*, 1988.

Other war-related: none.

Post-War career: Teaching and living Dunoon, Argyll. Lengthy trips teaching abroad: Kabul, Borneo, Barcelona. Prolific novelist.

ROBIN JENKINS was born in 1912 in Flemington, near Cambuslang in Lanarkshire. It was a small mining village, where 'pit bings rose like volcanoes out of fields and woods', and poverty and deprivation were commonplace. His father went to war, and came back in 1919, but died soon after of rheumatic fever. Jenkins and his siblings were brought up by their widowed mother in very straitened working-class circumstances, the best (fictionalised) account of which can be found in *Happy for the Child* (1953). Academically gifted, he went from Hamilton Academy to Glasgow University, where he read English, and proceeded to Teacher Training College, always straining to express himself as opposed to what he constantly found was a deadening conventionality of opinion and hierarchy. He began teaching at Strathclyde Primary in 1937, and it was with children from that slum area of Glasgow that he took his part in the 'phoney' war, accompanying young evacuees to the posh spa town of Moffat. When he was duly called up, he faced two tribunals as a (non-religious) conscientious objector, and was offered the alternative of working in agriculture or forestry. Not long married, he went into forestry for six long years, 1940–46: 'they kept us out quite a long time, you know, a full year longer than we needed to, I thought a bit vindictive, but in the end I came back and went into Riverside Senior Secondary School.' [1]

I quote him in the Spark chapter being congratulated on making so much of his forestry experience in his fiction:

> And I said look, if I had been at the war, it would have
> been a damn sight better thing for me. If I had managed to
> remain alive, I could have made a lot more of the war than
> of Forestry. (SWT 3 p 117)

But he was a novelist who wrote only from scenes grounded in some way in his personal experience, so like Spark he felt unqualified to treat World War Two because of his physical absence. As a result, that war as a historical reality is uncommon in his books, and *Guests of War* (1956) is the only novel that can be said to deal directly with it, while *Fergus Lamont* (1979) has a good deal to say about the previous war.

As an individual, Robin Jenkins was tormented by the horrors and paradoxes of war, and he repeatedly returned to these topics in his novels. I'll start with what he said to Bob Tait and myself in 1985, when we asked about his conscientious objection:

> I keep reading now about how this was a good war, about how this was a war to destroy evil. Now I wasn't concerned about objecting to this war or that war, I was objecting to war: I'm still objecting to war. And they've now got the danger of a greater war than ever; it's simply a lack of trust: and nobody, nobody anywhere, is trying to build up trust.
>   … I'm forgiving nobody for things like Dresden, Hiroshima, and the concentration camps: I forgive nobody for these things. (SWT 3 pp 117-9)

Jenkins was a conscientious objector who refused to plead a religious case: he had no religion. But he was adamantly opposed to war, particularly to indiscriminate slaughter. He went on to write more than twenty novels in the next fifty years, in many of which, inevitably, war figures. He saw himself as a rigid moralist. I wondered whether a man with such fixed and dogmatic opinions as Jenkins could tackle the subject without betraying his outrage at war, and his message of refusal, and found he could, by his means of presentation, which are crucial.

When I sought his permission to publish sections of our interviews in a special number of *Cencrastus* in 1985, he refused. He wrote:

> Thank you for the transcript of my haverings. I am afraid however that I would rather not have published such a baring of my soul, delivered in off-the-cuff, not very coherent remarks! I still stick to my position that all I want known of my private self is to be found in my novels.

In other words, he was not intending to publish or allow to be published personally formed dogma, or diatribes against war: he had considered long and hard what his books were to 'say' about war, and he was not concerned with sermons. (After accepting this judgment for many years, I decided to publish the whole interview. Jenkins' use of irony can confound the novel reader, leaving questions, and I feel his interview clears up a number of them.) The books would and do pose awkward and uncomfortable questions about this hot potato of a subject, such as might cause the reader positive discomfort. We have to read carefully, aware of whose thoughts we are receiving, and of shifting point of view, and of irony, and prepared to be critical.

I intend to leave out the novel of his which is most obviously concerned with conscientious objection, A Would-Be Saint (1979), because in that book we are also repeatedly faced with some dogmatic and idiosyncratic opinions about God and Christianity and sanctity from the fiercely agnostic novelist. This makes for a strange and fascinating novel, but doesn't, as far as I'm concerned, clarify Jenkins' own personal reasons for opposing war. (SWT 3 pp 117-22) But despite ruling himself out as chronicler of the last war, Jenkins writes over and over again about war in the abstract, or the idea of war. In fact, war is a central metaphor in his books, often the war between different ways of life, or the war of conflicting ideas or duties inside a character. Cairns Craig has declared:

> No modern Scottish novelist has presented so many aspects
> of Scottish society with such incisive concern for its inner
> conflicts and contradictions. [2]

So the book I intend to centre on is Guests of War (1956). First I will look briefly at two later novels, Fergus Lamont and Just Duffy. I will argue that in none of these do we find a simple anti-war message: that is not what novels do, and certainly not what Jenkins' novels do! These cover quite a time span. Fergus Lamont was published in 1979, and Bob Tait and I chose to treat it in Ten Modern Scottish Novels (1984), describing it as a peculiarly Scottish modern version of Dickens' Great Expectations.[3] It is the autobiography of the eponymous hero, almost all told in the first person, uniquely in Jenkins' work. It is an extraordinary achievement, because the central character and crucially unreliable narrator is quite extraordinary, 'generally preposterous, often repellent and probably crazed'.[4] Fergus is egotistical to an extraordinary degree, and blinds himself to any realities that might get in his way, as he decides to fulfil the predestined role of a born aristocrat and great poet, not to mention in some ineffable way being the predestined future 'saviour' of his native Gantock and the slums where he was reared. But through the mists of his benighted attitudes, we can discern some realities that he does not manage to distort. Two of these realities are his primary school classmates, Smout McTavish and Mary Holmscroft. Both of these are fellow slum dwellers, and their lives – and in particular their wars – are very different from Fergus's. They all lived through the Great War. Fergus's war is a matter of calculation and deception, passing himself off as an aristocrat, and seeing war in terms of career furtherance. 'The war would be pointless if I could not make use of it to distinguish myself'. He wins the MC for courage, but explains why he never believed he would be killed: self-elected to grace, he writes, 'I felt I had a genius in me, too valuable to be lost.' (p 95) Smout and Mary matter more, slightly more, to Fergus than any of the many other characters. Smout is seen first as a little boy hiding the large hole in the seat of his trousers as they play in the street, and it is Smout who asks to try on the garish yellow-and-black kilt that Fergus's romantic and suicidal mother clothed him in just before her death. He vows that one day he, Smout, will wear a kilt too. Smout leaves school early and becomes an errand boy, and an admirer of the beautiful but slightly soft Jessie McFadyen who already has a reputation for sexual over-generosity. At the outbreak of the Great War, Smout volunteers at once, and gets his kilt, but even his neighbours voice doubts:

> They were fond of him, they had brought him presents,
> but they could not help letting it be known that in their
> view there were hundreds of men in Gantock with far
> more reason than he to be grateful to king and country.
> They had big villas to defend, he a single-end. [...] Thus
> they reasoned, aloud, but it was obvious they were proud

of him for going before his turn. There being no word in
their vocabulary for a hero who was also a mug, they were
obliged to season their admiration with disapproval. (p 75)

It never occurs to Smout to question the ethics of war, or the slogan
that king and country needed him, and Jenkins allows him full respect
in the novel, despite his inevitable end as cannon fodder. In a late
return to Gantock, a much older Fergus stands by the war memorial
on which Smout and many other schoolmates are remembered, and
tries to conjure up Smout:

> I had tried to conjure him up as the shy twenty-one-year-old
> volunteer with the very short haircut who had so defiantly
> kissed Jessie McFadyen in the station, but I had not known
> that Smout very well. It was the skinny-shanked, solemn,
> patient, little Smout with the holes in his breeks who came
> and stood beside the angel.
>   I asked his advice.
> It was the same as it had always been. Be grateful for what
> you've got; or, in the words of a hymn that the Salvation
> Army used to sing at our street corner, and in which he had
> joined enthusiastically, to the consternation of all of his
> friends: 'Count your blessings'. With his ragged clothes,
> and his mother preferring to talk to the dead and play whist
> rather than sew or cook, he had struck us as having very
> few blessings of his own to count. Yet no one had ever heard
> him whine with envy or self-pity. (p 181)

Smout then asks Fergus to look after Jessie, which Fergus promises
to do, but to no one's surprise he fails even to attempt this. Smout
is basically used as a comparative measure to Fergus, but in his
brief but memorable presentation Jenkins attempts to show that
he is indeed a hero, by any standard. In an unpublished part of our
interview, he said:

Yes, *the* heroes of our time. A man like Smout, born and
brought up in a single-end and goes off to fight for his
country. That to my mind is most heroic. I can understand
if you've got a stately home and thousands of acres going
away to fight for them, but Smout! In spite of my views
I didn't take anything away from Smout: I gave him his
heroism, I hope.

Fergus' other early classmate Mary Holmscroft is a far simpler case,
because Jenkins, like Dickens, obeys the convention that however
idiosyncratic the narrator, quoted speech is to be taken as reliable,
and also characters' writing. Mary came from a much worse slum
than Fergus, but was rescued by a socialist teacher, and went to the
same senior school as Fergus. She outdoes him effortlessly in all
directions, despite his slanted misinterpretations of her motives and
his repeated betrayals. Thus we see directly that where Fergus is a
vain, hypocritical humbug, Mary is an honest socialist, dedicating
her life to improving life for the slum-dwellers. So she goes to Spain
at the outbreak of Civil War, and goes on to preach pacifism at the
outbreak of world war, and at last becomes an MP. Too perfect and
selfless, maybe, as a character herself, but the perfect foil to Fergus.

The problem of war and atrocity is a central one that the eponymous
hero of *Just Duffy* (1988) cannot resolve. The ambiguity of the title
sums it up: is he just Duffy, like *Just William*, a difficult boy? Or is he
the only person in his world who truly sees justly, a just judge?

Duffy is not his own narrator, as Fergus is, so as often with Jenkins
we have to be aware of the point of view our narrator is inhabiting,
from moment to moment. Most people think Duffy is simple-minded,
and he plays up to this. But people who realise there is more to him
than meets the eye tend to think that he is therefore very clever. He
is bright, but his humanity is lacking: one telling point is that he has
absolutely no sense of humour. The details of his story need not
concern us here – suffice it to say that his absolutist view of things,
carried forward with stubborn logic, leads him to murder and final
silence. It is almost as if Jenkins himself, minus his saving sense of
irony, were on trial.

But the reader, especially on first reading, finds it hard to fault his logic, or answer his dogmatic statements. So the novel constantly involves the reader in refuting wildly absurd logicalities, or accepting dire contradictions. Duffy has a consuming interest in war. He has read an encyclopaedia, and a history of war. He cannot understand the paradox that if a country declares war, suddenly all sorts of formerly atrocious actions becomes permissible. As Tom Leonard puts it in his modern Scots version of the Commandments, the command to do no murder becomes, 'nay g.b.h. (septina wawr).'[5] We realise we are hardly dealing with psychological realism when he asks a primary school teacher, in his perfect English: 'Duffy had asked Mr Flockhart if history books told the truth.' The answer he gets is hardly predictable in a primary class:

> 'Truth, Duffy, isn't simple. It looks different according
> to the angle you view it from. Some historians think the
> covenanters were irresponsible fanatics, others say they
> were godly men fighting for their rights. Russian historians
> don't take the same view of the Second World War that
> British historians do. We all believe what we want to believe,
> whether we're professional historians or school janitors.'
>   Duffy understood all that but he still believed that truth,
> at its core, was simple. (p 16)

What's more, he compiles a catalogue of human depravities, and reflects on them:

> Duffy was well aware that though most human beings
> were capable of atrocities very few committed them and
> the great majority condemned them utterly: except, of
> course, if they were done to win a war. No one cared how
> many babies or cats were burnt to death in Hiroshima or
> Dresden. (p 17)

When Duffy takes action, at first it is both serious and absurd. He declares war on the town, thus to his mind justifying his actions.

Under cover of night he inscribes these words on the town hall: 'WAR IS DECLARED ON DEFILERS OF TRUTH AND ABUSERS OF AUTHORITY'. With a gang of semi criminal youths and intense seriousness he proceeds to action: first they break into the library at night, and tear a page out of as many books as possible. Then they break into the town's smartest church and smear human excrement on the minister's Bible and the pew-holders' hymnbooks. This book is evidence indeed that Jenkins never gave up worrying about the issues raised by war.

Guests of War (1956) is based on a situation in which the novelist found himself in real life:

> I *did* go with Strathclyde Primary School kids to Moffat, and quite a lot of the things that happen in the book did happen in real life. Pretty much as I describe it, too. It was hilarious! (SWT3 p 138)

Naomi Mitchison heard about it at the time, and notes in her war diary:

> Some are back already. They were evacuated to Moffat which didn't want them a bit; two thirds had to be compulsorily billeted; all had passed their medical but the Moffat doctors turned back sixteen. Glasgow say they are perfectly all right and are furious. One boy said by one doctor to have ringworm, by another not: same with impetigo: same with dirty heads.

Angus Calder records that one MP wrote to the minister in charge: 'Compulsory billeting would be far worse than world war.' [6]

Here Jenkins uses a wider canvas, with many more characters, and on many levels it is a magnificently successful comic novel. And it comprises at least three wars. The first is the obvious one: evacuation was one of the main preliminaries to the outbreak of hostilities, and in Glasgow as in other places, it was a massive operation which later began to peter out when the expected bombs failed to appear. At the end of the novel:

> Those evacuees who still remained in that outpost of duty among the frosted hills were no longer bound in comradeship by the two-fold danger, from Hitler the outside enemy, and from the native Langrigg snobs. Gowburgh and other cities in Britain had not after all been bombed, and, it now seemed, never would be. More than half therefore had fled back home. (p 247)

But the centre of the book's comedy is a concentration on the other war:

> Remember war is about to be waged, not between Great Britain and Germany, but between ourselves and the inhabitants of Langrigg's cottages, villas, mansions and miniature castles. (p 18)

This is a major war in the book, the class war that erupts between the slum-dwellers of Gowburgh and the well-off middle-class dwellers of Langrigg, with evacuees, the Guests of War of the title. Jenkins' achievement here is to turn his satiric attention to both sides, favouring neither exclusively, but empathising with each in turn. The book is full of comic set-pieces – bathnight in Gowburgh before the exodus, the procession to the train, the chaotic scene of arrival at Langrigg, the catastrophe the Langriggians make out of billeting the evacuees, and so on. Here is a small extract from Gowburgh's procession to the station:

> But not only was the procession cheerful, it even went fey. A small man, who looked like a professional backcourt entertainer, appeared at the front with a set of aged bagpipes and led the way with defiant skirling tunes. It was clear he was playing for love; he would not pass his cap round for pennies. Boys whooped like Redskins; three of them dashed ahead

into a shop that sold penny whistles, and fell in behind the piper. Girls lifted their heads. Babies howled lustily. Mothers, wishing to scold and weep and grieve sorely enough to satisfy even Mr Grahamstone, were surprised into laughter. Few in that march were immune. (p 48)

But the teachers were different: the headmaster, Mr Grahamstone, 'persisted in walking as if behind a hearse: it was not perversity, but duty.' (p 48) Other teachers followed suit:

> Miss Oldswan, reverent in black coat and white hair, chided gently but unremittingly. Miss Cairncross, terror of diminutive delinquents, towered there among them like an Amazon paying stern penance for the many warriors she had slain. Mr Scoullar wore an expression that caused even Mr Grahamstone who approved of it to look unguardedly for the Bible under his oxter: it was an authentic going-to-Communion expression. (p 49)

Meantime, in Langrigg, the invasion reception awaits:

> On this fine day at the beginning of September, 1939, as the leading men of Langrigg waited in the little railway station to deal with this latest invasion, their task was more difficult because more complicated than any their predecessors had faced. If an invader was foreign and came with weapons, driving him back might be bloody and dangerous; but to do it was a clear duty, sanctioned by God, applauded in churches, and practised universally, even among the aborigines of Australia, those most backward of men. On the other hand, if the invaders were native, and came with uncouth but recognisable tongues, possible dirt, probable vermin, indisputable noise, and government permits, the problem of reception could not be so instinctively solved. (p 57)

The whole disastrous reception process is brilliantly conveyed, but not without empathy for the unwanted, the many-childed, the rejects. Fat Nan Ross accompanied by her six children are the most often rebuffed. As Longmate has it, 'Even less welcome than expectant mothers were women with small children.'[7] In the end, most of these will be housed in an empty mansion, Cairnban, under the care of our heroine, ordinary-looking fifty-year-old Bell McShelvie, mother of five, who has been mutely suffering the Gowburgh slums and pining for the countryside of her childhood for all her adult life. Before the pantomime involved in discovering Cairnban has no lighting, no furniture and no food, here is just one incident from the allocation: when, against all the rules, Mrs Rouster arrives at the billeting site:

> 'I want two little girls,' she said, and indicated the height
> required with her lavender-gloved hand. 'They must be
> clean, obedient, quiet, well-spoken, house and bed trained,
> and without a criminal pedigree.'

When gallant young teacher Roy pretends to 'serve' her, she wants to look for herself:

> 'That's why I am here, young man. I know very well I ought
> not to be. I know the fools got up some idiotic regulation
> about not allowing people to come and choose their
> own. My own husband was one of those fools. I happen
> to believe, however, that in a free country, which thank
> God ours still is' – here she gave Roy a look which asked
> more rudely than words why he was not being eviscerated
> somewhere to preserve that freedom – 'though not perhaps
> for much longer,' she went on, 'seeing how the fools have as
> usual blundered into war without being prepared for it – I
> happen to believe that we are entitled to refuse to harbour
> scoundrels, actual or potential. Gowburgh has a vile
> reputation.' (pp 88-9)

Vengefully, the mischievous Roy swops her two nice, ringleted little girls for the Baxter brothers, the worst of a rough bunch. 'She had collapsed into a chair with bouncy springs, and screamed, with her lavender-gloved hands flying on and off her eyes, like butterflies off flowers.' But when she manages to insult the Baxters – a hard task – they react:

> It went on till the Baxter pride was hurt, and the Baxter truculence roused. She used the one word of opprobrium they could not stomach. Inured to every monosyllabic obscenity, tolerant of such terms as riff-raff, scum, rubbish, midden-rakers, hooligans, and dirt, they had from babyhood been taught to resent with teeth and nails, with sticks and stones, and with retaliatory abuse, the appellation guttersnipe. It alone with mystical sharpness could find its way through their tough defences to their tender souls: to suffer it, and not object, whoever the inflictor, was to surrender their birthright as Gowburghians, as Scotsmen, as human beings, as children of God. 'For Christ's sake, missus,' yelled young Tom, 'shut your bluidy mooth.' And out of the house he raced, followed by Willie, who, passing the ship's bell that hung in the hall, clanged it as if to signify war was declared. (p 117)

As to the third kind of war, Jenkins' major characters often suffer inner wars: war is ironically his favourite metaphor for inner conflict. The 'wars' suffered here are principally two, those of Mrs Aldersyde and Bell McShelvie. Mrs Aldersyde's is a major war, one that she is destined to lose. This unattractive woman has been embittered by her struggle to spoil and promote her beautiful twins, to a point where she despises and abuses her hard-working husband and her fellow slum-dwellers, and disowns the war her country embarks on:

> What right has he telling us we're at war with the Germans? I've got no spite against them. They never did me any harm. But there are folk in Gowburgh I hae a spite against. My war's against them. (p 199)

She goes stridently to Langrigg, hoping somehow to stay with her children, demanding the headmaster accommodate her, but is finally humbled, having to take up Bell's earlier spurned offer to share her room at Cairnban that night with her and her daughter (the son wants none of it). They talk a while after all the children are asleep, and Bell has hopes that her attitudes are softening, but Mrs Aldersyde's last word is on her husband, and leaves Bell discouraged:

> 'He had no right to marry and bring children into the world when he wasn't fit for it.'
>   There was then, Mrs McShelvie knew, to be no complete redemption, no cleansing and healing of the wound. A little humility had been learned, and might as soon as tomorrow be forgotten. (p 219)

Bell McShelvie is the principal character, a middle-aged, rather plain woman who guiltily yearns for the possibility of accompanying the evacuees and staying with them in Langrigg as a helper. A neighbour accuses her of attempting to run away, and Bell, who always sees her own actions in the worst possible light, agrees from the start: her younger children will not need her as much as her rather frail husband and her flighty eldest daughter at home:

> Here indeed was her battlefield: the enemy she had to fight was despair at the ugliness shutting her in, at the inevitable coarseness and pitiable savagery of many of the people shut in with her, and above all at her inability to keep her own family healthy, sweet, and intact. She was weary of fighting. Even soldiers in war were given relief. But Isaac was not well, although he had started work; he might soon die, and all the sooner if she forsook him. Flora, with her lipstick, dancing, tawdriness of mind, and resentment at having to work to help bring up her brothers and sisters, might grow up to be little better than a prostitute; she needed, as Meg said, more control now rather than less. The battle was at its height, and she had made up her mind to desert. (p 11–12)

Bell is a very stern judge of herself, and easier on others – much like
Jenkins the novelist, indeed. In her view, Langrigg is a test which she
dismally fails, but the reader is unlikely to agree. True, her position
as 'warden' of Cairnban eventually tempts her to see herself as rather
above the rest, but what she sees as her punishment is out of all
proportion. This is the accidental death of her son Sammy, who was
widely recognised as special, although neither clever nor handsome:

> Some said he was too soft in the head [...], and sniggered at
> his bespectacled simplicity; but most admitted the softness,
> and greenness, were in his heart. As a substitute for those
> meadows and hills, Sammy all his twelve years had sufficed.
> (p 7)

Bell had longed like other parents for an outstandingly gifted child,
'through whom she could make contact with that ampler, brighter,
more lovely life which went on in the world outside the back streets
of Gowburgh.' (p 281) But her children were all ordinary. Sammy
is the uncertain factor in this analysis: from one point of view he is
an ungainly, bespectacled dunce, from another, one of the elect, a
spreader of happiness everywhere, a comfort, solace and absolution
to young Roy, a window to something better for Bell herself.

But unlike Mrs Aldersyde, Bell learns the lessons of her experience,
and comes to a new and maturer view. It has been her ambition to
climb Langrigg's local hill, Brack Fell. As she struggles in her ascent,
she comes to a decision about the resolution she will make at the
top:

> All along she had been aware of her treason. Before it
> was too late, she must make amends to the folk she had
> betrayed. Returning to Gowburgh would do, but only if she
> returned cleansed and unresentful, prepared to create as
> much light as she could, not only for herself and her family,
> but for her neighbours. (pp 282–3)

She has to do more; she has to admit to herself that she cannot reach the summit in time to return safely. So she turns back down the mountain. Fergus Lamont's notion of returning to the slums of Gantock with a redeeming love was risible and pathetic: Bell's quiet and unobtrusive return to her city will be silently heroic and effective. She ends up on the road back to her friends:

> She no longer saw defeat or disappointment, but only a
> necessary resolution.
>   As she plodded along the road her feet stung and her
> whole body ached; but she was smiling, with the tears
> running down her cheeks. (p 286)

So, given that none of the major characters questions the necessity of the war, does anyone utter what we might expect Jenkins to utter in the book on the question of war and the justness of fighting? Well, yes, but brilliantly Jenkins puts the denunciation in the mouth of a cynical, unlikeable older teacher, with whom the reader does not want to agree, as he attacks young Roy, who is only waiting for his call-up to the RAF. This is Campbelton, who has pretended for years that he has an honourable war wound from the Great War, although in fact it is only the result of falling over a bucket in the latrine. The gentleness of tone here might almost come from Jenkins himself, who loves his characters almost to the degree he thinks them mistaken. The child Jenkins had a father who was 'a machine-gunner, by god!' There is undoubted truth in what the older teacher says here, but his speech is infected or affected by his selfish cynicism, so fails to have its full impact in context.

> 'We are about to enter a slavering, snottery, gnashing,
> bloody, excremental, universal, madness, dear boy,' he
> said gently. 'I refer, of course to war. It will not do to gird
> on your sword, like Sir Galahad, and rush off to slay the
> ogre responsible for it all. You will achieve your ambition,
> Edgar, and become the pilot of an aeroplane. You will cross
> to Germany with a load of bombs and drop them to the

best of your ability upon some munition work, but really
they will fall on tenements filled with women and children
similar to those at present detained in the school. ... You
will fight the good fight, in the twentieth-century style. You
may become a hero, with medals. But, bless you, you will
never be Sir Galahad, who slew only ogres and on whose
soul consequently there was not to be found one blemish.'
(p 105)

So when reading Jenkins, we must consider not only the sentiments
expressed, but the character, viewpoint, and sometimes intelligence
of the person who expresses them, and what the reader can make of
them. And on a troubling question like war, the reader can expect to
come away somewhat troubled.

NOTES

1. Quoted from Isobel Murray, ed, *Scottish Writers Talking 3*, 2006, p 124. Further page numbers will be given in the text as (SWT 3 p 000)

2. Cairns Craig, 'Robin Jenkins – A Would-be Realist?', *Edinburgh Review 106*, p 12.

3. See Isobel Murray and Bob Tait, *Ten Modern Scottish Novels*, Aberdeen University Press, 1984, pp 194-218.

4. See Bob Tait's Introduction to the Canongate Classics edition of *Fergus Lamont*, 1990, p x.

5. Tom Leonard, 'Feed Ma Lamz' in *Intimate Voices: Selected Work 1965-1983*, Etruscan, 2003, p 46.

6. Naomi Mitchison, *Among You Taking Notes*, p 138; Calder, p 42.

7. Norman Longmate, *How We Lived Then: A History of Everyday Life During the Second World War*, Hutchinson, 1971, p 58.

MURIEL SPARK
and *The Girls of Slender Means*

Dates: 1918–2006.

Youth and Pre-War: Born and raised in Edinburgh; went to marry in Africa.

WW2: From 1944, worked in Intelligence at Milton Bryan.

Novels: *The Girls of Slender Means*, 1963; *The Hothouse By the East River*, 1973.

Other War-related: Autobiography, first volume (all published), *Curriculum Vitae*, 1992.

Post-War: Full time writer, living in London, USA and Italy.

MURIEL SPARK wrote an entertaining short story called 'The First Year of My Life' (1975). It purports to accept a psychological theory that babies are 'born omniscient'. Spark was born in 1918, 'the very worst year that the world had ever seen so far.' [1] In her account, the baby, conscious of world events, refused to smile.

> The Western Front on my frequency was sheer blood, mud, dismembered bodies, blistered crashes, hectic flashes of light in the night skies, explosions, total terror. Since it was plain I had been born into a bad moment in the history of the world, the future bothered me, unable as I was to raise my head from the pillow and as yet only twenty inches long.
> (pp 304–5)

She goes on: 'The strongest men on all fronts were dead before I was born... I checked my toes and fingers, knowing I was going to need them.' Nothing could persuade this all-too-aware baby to smile, until Mr Asquith said in parliament: 'All things have become new. In this great cleaning and purging it has been the privilege of our country to play her part.' This story is pure Spark, in its paradox and comic drive on the most serious of subjects. But in her novels, the subject virtually disappears.

It was not until I came to reread the novels of Muriel Spark with treatment of the war as a central interest that I noticed how few of her novels so much as mentioned the war. With two exceptions, which I will return to, war is mentioned only occasionally as a marker of time – 'before the war' or of place – 'parked beside the bombed-out building'. This promising young novelist enjoyed some of her own prime in London in the fifties, and part of the energetic effectiveness of her novels was their really contemporary atmosphere, never looking backward. This could perhaps be explained by the writer's absence from London for much of the war, but seems to apply to her characters too.

Memento Mori (1959), for example, is set in fifties London and famously deals with a number of very old people who are pursued by a telephone message: 'Remember you must die.' All of them have survived the war, even if they had no part in it, and we might assume those years might figure in their consciousness of the past – we might expect their histories to raise it, but no. Only Godfrey's son, a spoilt ne'er-do-well, was called up for war service, we are told late in the book, but was 'turned down on account of his psychological history.' (p 197) Spark's choice of focussing closely on her theme, here the old turning away from the awareness of the increasing proximity of death, means there are virtually no other middle-aged characters in the book. Again, *Loitering with Intent* (1981) is a novel in which the young writer Fleur Talbot, engaged on her first novel, *Warrender Chase*, takes a job ghostwriting the autobiographies of a bizarre group called the Autobiographical Association. But again, the war hardly gains a mention, although Fleur is confident that she can supply any necessary details without the relevant experience:

> I invented for my Warrender a war record, a distinguished one, in Burma, and managed to make it really credible even although I filled in the war bit with a very few strokes, knowing, in fact, so little about the war in Burma. It astonished me later to find how the readers found Warrender's war record so convincing and full when I had said so little – one real war veteran of Burma wrote to say how realistic he found it – but since then I've come to learn for myself how little one needs, in the art of writing, to convey the lot, and how a lot of words, on the other hand, can convey so little. (p 84)

But on the whole Muriel Spark did not choose to illustrate her character's confident claims: it is not until you look for the war that you find how absent it is from these books. Only in *A Far Cry From Kensington* (1988) does war inevitably take a small part, as its remarkable heroine Mrs Hawkins is introduced as a young war widow, and its main victim Wanda Podolak is a Polish refugee. We hear only a page or so about the late Mr Hawkins, and that far on, when we are more interested in Mrs Hawkins's next amorous adventure, and we never get details of Wanda's past in Poland, and how and why she left, before her life and death in London.

The situation became only more interesting in 1992, when Spark published her first and (as it turned out) only volume of autobiography, *Curriculum Vitae*. There she was concerned to sketch aspects of her life from her birth in 1918 as far as 1957, carefully correcting false impressions and erroneous attributions, but also interestingly confirming that some particular phases of her life came to be used in her fiction:

> Most of the memorable experiences of my life I have celebrated, or used for a background in a short story or novel. [2] (p 120)

This claim was a little startling, for two reasons: one, she was a very private person, and cloaked her private life in a secrecy that no one, including herself, was to disturb; and two, we are accustomed to thinking of her as perhaps *the* anti-realistic novelist, whose characters and situations are playfully and sometimes savagely created and manipulated in a kind of antithesis of 'real life'. But the novelist makes clear often in the autobiography that in some sense, however tenuous, her work is related to her personal experience. For example, mentioning *Loitering with Intent*, she writes: 'I transferred a number of my experiences in the Poetry Society, as I usually do, into a fictional background.' (p 134) She even writes:

> I had always been aware of 'gaining experience' for some future literary work. No experience, I felt, was to be overlooked, even that of my darkest hours in Africa. (p 154)

If she did follow this practice, it is by no means always detectable! What did she make of her childhood and teens? Although *The Prime of Miss Jean Brodie* (1961) is to my mind undoubtedly a masterpiece, it hardly encapsulates the worlds of Spark to the age of nineteen, when she got engaged to be married and travelled alone to Africa. And she wrote little of Africa, except a few fine short stories, and nothing of her unhappy marriage with an unstable husband and the birth of her son – indeed, even in *Curriculum Vitae* she is very brief on all that. On the whole, she firmly eschewed any obvious elements of autobiography in her fiction, and never wrote about the deeply personal aspects of her life: what she uses, it seems, is a version of what she observed in others: this tends to be what is utilised in the fiction. Most of her novels are set either in London in the fifties, in the USA or in various European settings, in a kind of timeless contemporaneity. Latterly, most of the characters are rich and many of them superficial, and servants, who figure largely, tend to be venal, clever and successful. There is a lot of blood. Spark observed in 1970 that in an age of absurdity she wanted literature to shed feelings and generosity, and to devote itself to satire and ridicule. [3]

But the big time gap remains the war. One obvious and sufficient reason is Spark's absence from the United Kingdom: she was away in Africa from August 1937 to March 1944. It is clear that she later regretted this, and was keen to make up for it. In *Curriculum Vitae*, she says 'I escaped for dear life'. (p 132) She was 'now determined to see wartime England. I wanted to be involved'. Although she was unable to bring her son, 'I decided for my sanity's sake to go ahead by myself.' (p 136) She 'escaped' on a troop-ship in late February 1944. And when she reached the UK, 'Believe it or not, I chose London rather than peaceful Edinburgh because I wanted to "experience" the war.' (p 143) This writerly eagerness to be a part of it reminds me inevitably of the long interview I had with Robin Jenkins in 1985. Jenkins was a conscientious objector and adamant in his principled opposition to war, and was therefore sent to spend the war in Argyll, working in forestry. He used this experience to great effect in several novels. When Bob Tait and I interviewed him at length in 1985 he recalled this wryly:

We had just been listening to George Blake's review of *The Cone-Gatherers* (1955) on the radio. One member of senior staff said to me in a friendly way... –'John, your being in forestry was a great thing for you. Look how you've used it in the books.' And I said 'look, if I had been in the war it would have been a damn sight better thing for me. If I had

managed to remain alive, I could have made a lot more of
the war than of forestry.' [4]

So Spark made the most of her one year of the war. It yielded the
settings and locations for two novels. One of these treated her unusual
and interesting war-work in Black Propaganda or Psychological
Warfare: this was *The Hothouse By The East River* (1973). She
worked for six months as a minor cog in a 'concentrated braintank'
(CV p 148) near Woburn, at Milton Bryan, and she describes it as
she remembered it in her autobiography, years after producing a very
singular version of it in that novel. She commuted to London for
long weekends twice a month, living in the Helena Club, which, she
tells readers, was the original of the May of Teck Club in an earlier
and more successful novel, *The Girls Of Slender Means* (1963). So
two novels ensued, using situations, elements of plot and character
from these experiences, reflecting, or perhaps distorting, her actual
experience: economy was one of her guiding principles.

The autobiographical account of Spark's war-work is clear and
straightforward. (CV pp 145–59) It involved trying to broadcast fake
propaganda to Germans who mistook it for a German service. They
had one great advantage:

> By enormous luck, we had a teleprinter directly connected
> to Goebbels' news transmitter in Germany... . The
> invaluable machine was known as the Hell-schreiber. (p 153)

For radio announcers they used German prisoners of war 'who had
agreed to work for us in a role in which, as truly patriotic Germans,
they could oppose Hitler and the Nazis'. (p 151) They were protected
by anonymity and promised British citizenship after the war. There
is no hint in Spark's account that this is not 'our' war: she never
questions the issues or alliances involved. So that these Germans are
not to be regarded as traitors, in any sense. Spark used to go for walks
with individuals from 'those brave POWs, who were risking so much
to smash Hitler'. (p 155) Spark relates an occasion when one of these
volunteered to speak to a German station to tell his family about

his safety. But it turned out that his voice could have been traceable, and this could have had severe repercussions in unmasking the fake identity of Radio Atlantic. In her autobiography, Spark suddenly adds here:

> I used this incident with fictional variations in my novel
> *The Hothouse By The East River*. There was something
> surrealistic, mysterious, about the affair, which I think the
> novel tones in with. (p 159)

Stannard's biography chronicles the delays in composition, summing up the author's difficulties as 'a seven-year burden'.[5]

The novel is very short and very surreal. Set in New York long after the war, it involves principally Elsa and her husband Paul, who both worked during the war at Milton Bryan. Elsa is massively rich, and reportedly mad: her shadow falls a different way from other peoples', a traditional sign of witchcraft. She spends most of her time gazing out of the windows at the river in an apartment that is insufferably hot, winter and summer. One day she claims to have re-encountered one of the German POWs from the war, one that Paul had had reimprisoned and who had reportedly died inside. Everything is liable to repetition, vagueness, possibility. It transpires at the end that Elsa and Paul were both killed by a V-2 bomb in 1944.

So the non-life of the novel represents a kind of afterlife. Not a traditional Hell, for all the heat, but a dry, secular repetition of meaninglessness. We get an early pointer to this:

> New York, home of the vivisectors of the mind, and of the
> mentally vivisected still to be reassembled, of those who
> live intact, habitually wondering about their states of sanity,
> and home of those whose minds have been dead, bearing
> the scars of resurrection: New York heaves outside the
> consultant's office, agitating all around her about her ears.
> (p 11)

The characters do not seem to be undergoing anything as definite as punishment, or to have committed anything as serious as the outdated notion of sin. The wartime treason issues are not taken seriously, nor the possibility of sexual transgression.

In contrast to contemporary New York, Paul tells his son Pierre:

> 'Listen to me,' his voice is saying... In the summer of 1944, he is telling his son, life was more vivid than it is now. Everything was more distinct. The hours of the day lasted longer. One lived excitedly and dangerously. There was a war on [...] 'We really lived our life.' (pp 29-30)

And much later the son Pierre tells his father:

> Spies don't matter any more.... . There isn't any war and peace any more, no good and evil, no communism, no capitalism, no fascism. There's only one area of conflict left and that's between absurdity and intelligence. (p 63)

This novel seems to belong more to the unhappy dark world of Spark's American novels, like its predecessors, *The Driver's Seat* (1970) and *Not To Disturb* (1971) than to the novels of 1950s London, like *The Girls of Slender Means* (1963).

The Hothouse By The East River is short, but *The Girls Of Slender Means* makes up an even slimmer volume. And where the former leaves us (me plus all the critics I've seen) in some doubt or confusion, the latter is a model of neatness, economy and simplicity. This is not to suggest it is shallow, far from it; at many levels it yields truths of clarity and suggestiveness. Even the title reads on at least two levels: the May of Teck Club exists for 'girls of slender means' who come to live in London for their work, and have little cash for accommodation; and the horrific climax of the novel occurs when a three-year-old unexploded bomb in the club garden inexplicably devastates the fire escape in 1945, trapping girls upstairs, so that for a while only agile girls with very slender hips can writhe through the only means of escape, a tiny lavatory window giving on to a flat roof outside.

The action of the novel takes place between VE Day in May 1945 and the public celebrations of VJ Day in August, after Hiroshima and Nagasaki, although they remain unmentioned. Spark exercises her well-known and very ingenious techniques of flash forward and flashback, and the time scheme is very tightly controlled. Its climax occurs the day after the General Election results were announced – a Labour landslide. The novel opens with an omniscient – but definitely personal – narrator surveying not only the scarred surface of London, but, perhaps, the spirit of May of Teck:

> Long ago in 1945 all the nice people in England were poor, allowing for exceptions. The streets of the cities were lined with buildings in bad repair or in no repair at all, bomb-sites piled with stony rubble, houses like giant teeth in which decay had been drilled out, leaving only the cavity. Some bomb-ripped buildings looked like the ruins of ancient castles until, at a closer view, the wallpapers of various quite normal rooms would be visible, room above room, exposed, as on a stage, with one wall missing; sometimes a lavatory chain would dangle over nothing from a fourth- or fifth-floor ceiling; most of all the staircases survived, like a new art-form, leading up and up to an unspecified destination that made unusual demands on the mind's eye. All the nice people were poor; at least, that was a general axiom, the best of the rich being poor in spirit. (p 7)

The celebration is of youth and poverty and 'niceness', although we are immediately introduced to 'bomb-ripped buildings', with what turns out to be a loaded image of staircases leading 'up and up'. The narrator continues:

> There was absolutely no point in feeling depressed about the scene, it would have been like feeling depressed about the Grand Canyon or some event of the earth outside everybody's scope.

The girls are introduced early, first generally: 'Their eyes gave out an eager-spirited light that resembled near-genius, but was youth merely.' This narrator demands our detailed attention! Then she (it is surely a she?) goes on to prophesy:

> As they realized themselves in varying degrees, few people alive at the time were more delightful, more ingenious, more movingly lovely, and, as it might happen, more savage, than the girls of slender means. (p 9)

By this time the narrator has thoroughly established herself as a guide to the general mood of the time, and has just indeed uttered a central paradox of the novel. She will go on, in different vein, to supply comments on all the characters, sometimes bitchy and always delicious, and the reader who chooses to ignore her guidance will surely flounder. Spark always insisted the narrator of each novel was not herself, the writer, but a character, and here the character is of great importance.

When the introductions are more particularized, the youngest girls in the dormitory on the first floor are undifferentiated, and remain so, inexperienced, convulsed with laughter at simple jokes. More individualized are those sharing rooms on the second floor, and on the third those condemned (self-condemned, it seems) to celibacy. The fourth and top floor contains most of the girls we come to know best. The exception to this is third-floor Joanna Childe, rector's daughter crossed in love by her own ideal of love, who has decided to 'enter maimed into the Kingdom of Heaven'. (p 25) She is a devoted elocutionist, and her loud declamations of often religious verse resound through the novel: she is mistaken by most for 'something emotionally heroic'. (p 25) But the narrator knows better:

> Joanna Childe had been drawn to this profession by her good voice and love of poetry which she loved rather as it might be assumed a cat loves birds; poetry, especially the declamatory sort, excited and possessed her; she would pounce on the stuff, play with it quivering in her mind,

and when she had got it by heart, she spoke it forth with devouring relish. (p 11)

If we attend to the narrator, we will not become uncritically attracted to any of the characters: Spark wants to engage our minds. Only the young poet Nicholas Farringdon understands, and 'almost' says, 'She is orgiastical in her feeling for poetry' (p 80), and 'Joanna needs to know more about life,… but if she knew life she would not be proclaiming these words so sexually and matriarchally as if in the act of suckling a divine child.' (p 86) So Joanna is doomed to be misunderstood by most, and to die a victim in an apparently heroic literary way.

But before I go on to the other girls, I must pause to ask, is this really in any meaningful sense a 'war novel'? The answer has to be a resounding yes. Wartime London is not just a backdrop to the novel: it is the central reality. What marks Joanna out in her capacity as a wartime civilian also marks every other character without exception, and that is how great a distance there is between her concerns and the fact of ongoing war. The novel is a typically ruthless Sparkian examination of civilian – especially young female civilian – reactions to the war which is determining life and death reality and the fates of nations. They treat war-damaged London and the ongoing war as backdrop to the fascinating minutiae of their own lives as did Bessie and Lily in Fred Urquhart's books.

Joanna is wrapt in poetry, and is 'entering maimed into the Kingdom of Heaven'. She did war work in her father's parish, but now, like all the others, having celebrated VE Day, ignores the war. She is unaware of the election, except for appraising Churchill's 'Sinaitic predictions' of a Labour government on the radio as a fellow professional. (p 86) No one seems very aware of the vast issues faced by the world, military and civilian. The dormitory girls are like all the others:

Love and money were the vital themes in all the bedrooms and dormitories. Love came first, and subsidiary to it was money for the upkeep of looks and the purchase of clothing coupons at the official black-market price of eight coupons for a pound. (p 26)

The dormitory girls at least have the excuse of being very young and living in an extended kind of boarding school: they are 'not yet experienced in discussing men'. (p 27) Their sense of time has had to adjust to rapidly disappearing boy friends and new ones by the week, an unnatural situation for anyone, and it remains distorted:

> The Air Force was mostly favoured, and a DFC was an
> asset. A Battle of Britain record aged a man in the eyes of
> the first-floor dormitory, in the year 1945. Dunkirk, too,
> was largely something that their fathers had done. It was
> the air heroes of the Normandy landing who were popular,
> lounging among the cushions in the drawing-room. (p 27)

As for slang, there is '"pressing on regardless". All the club, infected by the Air Force idiom current amongst the dormitory virgins, used this phrase continually.' (pp 44-5)

Jane Wright, who as a peerless 'woman columnist' phones round years later to relay the news of Nicholas Farringdon's martyrdom, has weightier problems to concern her, the most pressing being her own weight. Jane is fat, and obsesses about it. She therefore makes much of her literary career, what she calls her brainwork. She is employed by a shady publisher to get the better of his clients, and by a shady foreigner to attract holograph letters or at least signatures by writing fan letters to famous authors. Jane is fully convinced of her own frequent 'brainwaves', although the sometimes waspish narrator says flatly at one point that she has no intellect:

> It was not till Jane had reached the apex of her career as a
> reporter and interviewer for the largest of women's journals
> that she found her right role in life, while still incorrectly
> subscribing to a belief that she was capable of thought –
> indeed, was demonstrating a capacity for it. (p 72)

Her occupation produces regular rewards for the reader: when Nicholas Farringdon is martyred many years later, she still has all the girls' numbers. At intervals she breaks into the narrative to break this exciting news to her former neighbours. Their reactions are typical: Dorothy says, 'I'm shattered. I've got heaps to tell you.' Anne thinks, 'You could get a good story for your paper out of it.' Bookseller Rudi responds, 'Nick's dead? Hold on please, Jane. I have a customer waiting to buy a book.' And so on. If the May of Teck girls made an indelible mark on Nicholas Farringdon's life, he left no discernible mark on theirs.

The narrator warned at the start that,

> Few people alive at the time were more delightful, more ingenious, more movingly lovely, and, as it might happen, more savage, than the girls of slender means. (p 9)

The embodiment of savagery is the lovely Selina, with her 'long unsurpassable legs'. She is the most beautiful and the most coolly manipulative of all. While Joanna's rich recitations of *The Wreck of the Deutschland* may contain elements unkindly described as 'orgiastical', they pale beside Selina's twice daily recitation. While some Catholic might pause at noon daily, as Mrs Hawkins did in *A Far Cry From Kensington*, to recite the Angelus prayer, Selina solemnly recites the fruits of her correspondence course in Poise:

> Poise is perfect balance, an equanimity of body and mind, complete composure whatever the social scene. Elegant dress, immaculate grooming, and perfect deportment all contribute to the attainment of self-confidence. (p 50)

Selina can and does leave a scene of screaming panic with a naked girl stuck in a tiny window to repeat this mantra in her own room. (p 110) She sleeps variously with three weak men who attract but do not attempt to dominate her, while keeping an eye on a wealthy prospect she may marry, who probably will. Sexual success, rationing, hairpins and clothing coupons, Selina has no awareness of the war except as far as it provides her savage hunting ground.

All the slim girls on the top two floors vie for the loan of a very special ball dress, a stunning and colourful Schiaparelli model that was passed on to one of them by an aunt. It is memorable, and must not be worn too often where it might be remembered. When the novel comes to a climax, Selina steals the dress. Now, even a devout Catholic might demur that stealing a dress is perhaps not a mortal sin, but the circumstances here are very particular.

The slim girls had earlier all tried to get through the tiny lavatory window to sunbathe on the flat roof outside. Many had used scarce soap or margarine rations to grease their skin to fit, but few had managed through. Selina of course was an exception, and she pioneered a new use for the flat roof, making love there with Nicholas on the long summer nights. This window had been the only means of egress since the trapdoor in the bathroom ceiling was bricked up. This happened long before the war, when a man had entered and caused 'a legend of many screams in the night' (p 30), the exact explanation of which is lost in myth. Now it is 'a mere useless square'. The precariousness of top floor existence was now only alleviated by 'a back staircase leading down two flights to the perfectly sound fire-escape'. (p 31) Despite this, Selina made a remark which turned out to be true: 'If there was a fire, we'd be stuck.' When the bomb in the garden eventually explodes, it destroys this fire-escape, and many girls are trapped on the top floor, their only possible escape being the slit window, unless the emergency firemen can open up the trapdoor before the fire reaches them. In the event, Selina, Anne and Pauline slip through the window, and in a second desperate attempt Tilly gets through at the cost of a broken hip. The rest are left to panic beneath the trapdoor, with Joanna reciting 'the strange utterances of Day 27 in the Anglican order'.

But Selina goes back in:

> Nicholas immediately supposed she had done this in an attempt to rescue one of the girls, or assist their escape through the window.

> 'Come back out here, Selina, he shouted, [...] 'It's dangerous. You can't help anybody.' (p 122)

Then he sees her returning:

> She was carrying something fairly long and limp and
> evidently light in weight, enfolding it carefully in her arms.
> He thought it was a body. [...] It was the Schiaparelli dress.
> The coat-hanger dangled from the dress like a headless neck
> and shoulders. (p 125)

Now safely out with the dress, she leaves the scene to care for
the dress, not to return. As the effects of the explosion and the
resulting fire combine with the reverberations the firemen are
making on the roof, the panicking girls gradually scramble up a
proffered ladder:

> A whistle sounded as Joanna was half-way up. A voice from
> the megaphone ordered the men to jump clear. The house
> went down as the last fireman waited at the skylight for
> Joanna to emerge. As the sloping roof began to cave in, he
> leapt clear, landing badly and painfully on the flat roof-top.
> The house sank into its centre, a high heap of rubble, and
> Joanna went with it. (p 130)

Meantime, something strange and ambiguous is happening to
Nicholas:

> Later, reflecting on this lightning scene, he could not trust
> his memory as to whether he then involuntarily signed
> himself with the cross. It seemed to him, in recollection,
> that he did. At all events, Felix Dobell, who had appeared
> on the roof again, looked at him curiously at the time, and
> later said that Nicholas had crossed himself in superstitious
> relief that Selina was safe. (pp 125-6)

Is this an instant conversion, the kind of inspiration that motivated
Lord Marchmain on his deathbed in *Brideshead Revisited*? Nicholas
is nowhere presented as a knight in shining armour. Jane the publisher

knows him first as a (good-looking) poet and anarchist. His war
history turns out to be less than distinguished. Jane's shady friend
Rudi supplies the gossip:

> Before the war he had been always undecided whether
> to live in England or France, and whether he preferred
> men or women, since he alternated between passionate
> intervals with both. Also, he could never make up his
> mind between suicide and an equally drastic course of
> action known as Father D'Arcy [...] Nicholas was a
> pacifist up to the outbreak of war, Rudi said, then he
> joined the Army. Rudi said, 'I have met him one day in
> Piccadilly wearing his uniform, and he said to me the war
> has brought him peace. Next thing he is psychoanalysed
> out of the Army, a wangle, and he is working for the
> Intelligence'. (p 53)

After such conversations the narrator sums up, 'So much for the
portrait of the martyr as a young man'. (p 59) Wavering and
indecisive, self-dramatising, an unlikely candidate for sanctity. The
narrator confirms much of Rudi's story:

> Nicholas had been out of the Army since the month after
> Dunkirk, from which he had escaped with a wound in
> the thumb; his release from the army had followed a mild
> nervous disorder in the month after Dunkirk. (p 62)

But she also, early in the book, confirms the sign of his conversion:

> He had not yet witnessed that action of savagery so
> extreme that it forced him involuntarily to make an entirely
> unaccustomed gesture, the signing of the cross upon
> himself. (p 60)

What happens in the interim is that Nicholas, like Felix Dobell,
partly falls in love with the whole idea of the May of Teck club,

in all their niceness, poverty and loveliness. More particularly, he falls heavily for Selina, and wants to awaken her to his ideal:

> With the reckless ambition of a visionary, he pushed his passion for Selina into a desire that she, too, should accept and exploit the outlines of poverty in her life. He loved her as he loved his native country. He wanted Selina to be an ideal society personified amongst her bones, [...] It was not the first instance of a man taking a girl to bed with the aim of converting her soul, but he [...] willed the awakening of her social conscience. (p 92)

It is from this extreme and idealistic position that he witnesses her reality. It is after this that he goes to Haiti as a missionary and is martyred, long after he scribbled a note in his manuscript, 'that a vision of evil may be as effective to conversion as a vision of good.' (p 140)

One final point about *The Girls of Slender Means* is that it captures the crowd emotions of VE and VJ nights as I have never seen it done, except in the well known newsreels. I have described the novel's characters as largely disconnected from the war, but at the start the girls join the manic, depersonalised rejoicing of VE night wholeheartedly – and the celebration of the distant Royals:

> The whole club [...] had gone like swift migrants into the dark cool air of the park, crossing its wide acres as the crow flies in the direction of Buckingham Palace, there to express themselves along with the rest of London on the victory in the war with Germany. They clung to each other in twos and threes, fearful of being trampled. When separated, they clung to, and were clung to by, the nearest person. They became members of a wave of the sea, they surged and sang until, at every half-hour interval, a light flooded the tiny distant balcony of the Palace and four small straight digits appeared upon it: the King, the Queen, and the two Princesses. The royal family raised their right

arms, their hands fluttered as in a slight breeze, they were three candles in uniform and one in the recognisable fur-trimmed folds of the civilian queen in wartime. The huge organic murmur of the crowd, different from anything like the voice of animate matter but rather more a cataract or a geological disturbance, spread through the parks and along the Mall. [...] Many liaisons, some permanent, were formed in the night, and numerous infants of experimental variety, delightful in hue of skin and racial structure, were born to the world in the due cycle of nine months after. The bells pealed. Greggie observed that it was something between a wedding and a funeral on a world scale. (pp16–17)

The emphasis is on celebration, even if the crowd has a potential to scare in its 'huge organic murmur'. And there seems no hint of disapproval in the description of the carnivalesque celebrations. But by August and VJ night the emphasis has shifted, as the atom bombs have been dropped, and Nicholas and the reader have learned a little more about savagery. They have heard of Hiroshima and Nagasaki, but superficially it is the same: 'The public swelled on VJ night of August as riotously as on the victory night of May. The little figures appeared duly on the balcony every half-hour, waved for a space and disappeared.' (p 140) Jane is kissed by a seaman, 'at the mercy of his wet beery mouth', and then Nicholas sees something more sinister and equally inescapable:

Here, another seaman, observed only by Nicholas, slid a knife silently between the ribs of a woman who was with him. The lights went up on the balcony, and a hush anticipated the Royal appearance. The stabbed woman did not scream, but sagged immediately. Someone else screamed, through the hush, a woman, many yards away, some other victim. Or perhaps that screamer had only had her toes trodden upon. [...] Nicholas tried unsuccessfully to move his arm above the crowd to draw attention to the wounded woman. He had been shouting that a woman had been stabbed. The seaman was shouting accusations at his limp woman, who was still kept upright by the crowd. These private demonstrations faded in the general pandemonium. [...] It was a glorious victory. (pp 140–2)

Do we hear a distant echo of Mr Asquith's 'great cleaning and purging'?

NOTES

1. See The *Complete Short Stories* of Muriel Spark, 2001, pp 303–9.

2. *Curriculum Vitae*, 1992. Page references will be given in the text, with 'CV' only where source is not clear.

3. Muriel Spark: 'The Desegregation of Art' in *Proceedings of the American Academy of Arts and Letters*, 1971, pp 20–7.

4. See *Scottish Writers Talking 3*, ed, Isobel Murray, Edinburgh, 2006, p 117.

5. Martin Stannard, *Muriel Spark: The Biography*, 2009, p 385.

JESSIE KESSON
and *Another Time, Another Place*

Dates: 1916–1994.

Youth and Pre-War: Born Inverness Workhouse; raised in Elgin slums until removed at age ten to an orphanage at Kirkton-of-Skene. Married 1937: farm worker, mother. Early journalism.

WW2: Civilian farmworker: in 1943 Italian POWs sent to help on the farm and Kesson set to look after them. Writing for BBC.

Novel: *Another Time, Another Place*, 1983.

Post-War: Writer of novels and BBC plays; plus a series of hard, physical cleaning or caring jobs in London.

JESSIE KESSON was a civilian during the Second World War. She and her husband Johnny Kesson were farm-workers, moving from farm to farm every six or twelve months, living in small tied cottar houses on the farmers' land, often in a small, rather dysfunctional community, but separated not just from the war, but from the rest of society. The exception to this happened in 1943, when the Kessons were working in the Black Isle, and Italian prisoners of war were sent to work on the farm, and Kesson herself was appointed as their general caretaker and translator. For a time, the war invaded the farm. This is the factual, historical basis of *Another Time, Another Place* (1983). [1]

Kesson was born illegitimate in the Workhouse in Inverness in 1916. She constituted her mother's second 'mistake', and exhausted the patience of her grandfather, who had taken the first baby into his family. Now he washed his hands of her. Kesson was raised variously in the Model Lodging House in Elgin, and in slum properties, with her mother, whom she loved dearly, despite her having a real drink problem and engaging in small time prostitution. When the girl was ten, she was separated from her mother, who was accused of neglect, and she was sent to a small orphanage far away in Skene, Aberdeenshire. She would only see her mother once more before adulthood, when Liz, suffering from syphilis and losing her sight, visited the orphanage, to ask for her teenaged daughter to be allowed to go back to Elgin to nurse her, as she was going blind. This was refused.

Kesson settled in the orphanage, despite missing her mother, and did very well at school. But she was not allowed to proceed to university, because such an outcome was not customary, and in particular the Orphanage Trustees thought education would be wasted on a girl. She never ceased to regret and resent this.

After failing dismally at a number of dismal and menial jobs, at seventeen she attacked the Matron of her Aberdeen hostel, and spent a year in a mental hospital, another of a series of gifted women, from Florence Nightingale and Beatrice Webb to her personal heroine Virginia Woolf, who suffered a diagnosis of neurasthenia in their attempt to express their talents in the male-dominated world they found themselves in. [2]

She met and married her husband Johnny while recuperating from her illness, and together they were farm workers, 'cottaring' around the north east of Scotland from 1939 to 1951. She hated the conditions they worked in, the tied cottages, often in really poor condition, the two days off a year, the 'sack without words' if the farmer did not specifically ask his employee to stay on every six months. Meanwhile she began to write, and had her work published in magazines, and then broadcast by the BBC in Aberdeen.

In 1951, after the death of her mother in an Elgin institution, Kesson pioneered the family move to London with Johnny and the two children. She spent the second half of her life there. Now she combined a career as a radio dramatist with a bizarre series of often heavy jobs taken on to keep the family. She cooked and cared for old folk, did psychodrama with disturbed teenagers. hoovered a cinema and cleaned a nurses' home. She was by turns teacher, social worker, artist's model and radio producer. Small wonder she entitled the projected autobiography she never wrote *Mistress of None*. She died in 1994.

Even this brief summary of her life shows that on the whole the war did not loom large in it. She published a few poems about former schoolmates who were lost, but on the whole she spent the whole war as a cottar wife with literary aspirations. As always, she was an 'ootlin', deprived in her daily experience of any others who could share her literary interests and ambitions:

> Every work I've ever written contains ae 'ootlin'. Lovely
> Aberdeenshire word. Somebody that never really fitted into
> the thing… It's always aboot people who don't fit in! Now,
> I know mysel at last and it's just in one line in that book
> where fowk were oot who never had any desire to be in. [3]

The advent of these Italian prisoners of war was the only time the war touched Kesson directly, but it was something she wrote about at intervals over forty years. These versions include an openly autobiographical piece in *North-East Review* in 1944, shortly after their departure, describing the Italians vividly in their individuality, and describing good times with 'macaron'. There is a later long unpublished prose account (undated), called 'Another Place, Another Time', and a later radio play of 1980, all before the novel she wrote at white heat in 1983, fired by the film plans of Michael Radford, who had filmed *The White Bird Passes* in 1980. Her previous repeated handling of the material over the years meant that now she could write a seamless novella, with no problems of structure or time-shift: the use of three asterisks every few paragraphs to indicate a shift in time or scene is all that is required. Her later writing has matured magnificently.

All four of her short novels were the result of many rewrites and different versions. They often began as short accounts in *North-East Review* or *The Scots Magazine* of aspects of her own life: *The White Bird Passes* is the classic example here. Her first account of her troubled young life is given in 'Railway Journey', just a few short pages in *North-East Review* in 1942. It describes a girl's attempt to return to Elgin, to a community and a past from which she was brutally severed when she was sent to the orphanage. Sketches and tone and treatments varied over the years, as she recorded aspects of her youth in both Elgin and Skene, developing many into radio plays in the late 1940s. The final version of the novel was published in 1958, after a long and sometimes tortured relationship with the well-meaning directors of Chatto and Windus, whose suggestions often conflicted with her instinctive grasp of form and direction. In the end she turned aside to construct and publish a separate version of the ending as a short story. When she produced a version of this to the publishers it satisfied them, and at last herself. [4]

So, are we talking autobiography or fiction? We are in dangerous territory here. It is important to remember always that it is never safe to identify an author with her protagonist. Neither Janie in *The White Bird* nor the young woman in *Another Time, Another Place* in any meaningful sense 'equals' Kesson. Kesson of course was entitled to move between the personae occasionally as we are not. She wrote to her publisher Peter Calvocoressi about the *White Bird* heroine Janie (and by implication the young woman of the later novel), running the two together with part of her own experience:

> Janie at eighteen, married for two reasons, 'safety' and
> kindliness, and in doing so entered a No Man's Land, the
> only place she ever really fitted in to. Because it was vast and
> free of accident. And not sad in the *true* sense, except for
> loneliness sometimes.

We must remember that Janie is the last of at least fifteen constructed versions of Kesson's childhood, all notably different, and she is the one which most satisfied her author. But traditional literary criticism, contemporary theory and feminist criticism would all suggest the considerable dangers of simply identifying the author and her protagonist. David Copperfield was not Dickens, although they shared very painful childhood experiences. Ruskin wrote a vividly remembered autobiography, *Praeterita*, in which he did not include incidents that it gave him no pleasure to remember. He described its protagonist as 'the "natural" me – only peeled carefully'.

To the commentator on women's writing over the last two hundred years, there are special features in women writers' attempts at autobiography, whether presented as fiction or not. These are often women who have grown up seeking to measure themselves against, or to recognise themselves in, a largely male-engendered tradition, which, particularly in the nineteenth century, tended to polarise women into the sainted, sexually pure wife and mother, passive and incapable of sexual feelings, and the dangerous fallen woman, sexually experienced and seductive, threatening or even monstrous. Finding these reflections of herself inadequate, the woman writer has had to create a more adequate framework in which to construct her own identity. Linda Anderson writes about the difficulty:

> Inevitably autobiography as the way to write the self, or
> give the self a narrative, is deeply bound up with these
> questions or questionings of identity… . It is necessary to
> take into account the fact that the woman who attempts to
> write herself is engaged by the nature of the activity itself
> in re-writing the stories that already exist about her since
> by seeking to publicise herself she is violating an important

cultural construction of her femininity as passive or hidden. She is resisting or changing what is known about her. Her place within culture, the place from which she writes, is produced by difference and produces difference. The myth of the self which recent theorists have questioned may not be present for her in the same way; it is more difficult for her to believe in a self that can exist before writing, a self that is unified and continuous. Autobiography may self-consciously exist for her as an alternative place of identification. [5]

Clearly, this is especially true of Kesson's life, people and places suddenly snatched away, ideas of self and home shattered, new contexts repeatedly supplied into which she is required to fit. I have argued in the biography *Jessie Kesson: Writing Her Life* that the repeated attempts to remember or recreate the past were part of a process of establishing a self. [6]

These two novels, *The White Bird Passes* and *Another Time, Another Place*, published twenty-five years apart, concern protagonists who are clearly in some sense fictionalised 'versions' of Kesson, and both books share a sense of loss, of missed opportunities, of 'the grave of dreams'. The title of *The White Bird Passes* is taken from a poem by 'Fiona Macleod' called 'The Valley of White Poppies'. It could serve as an epigraph for both books:

> A white bird floats there like a drifting leaf:
> It feeds upon faint sweet hopes and perishing dreams
> And the still breath of unremembering grief.

> And as a silent leaf the white bird passes,
> Winnowing the dusk by dim forgetful streams.
> I am alone now among the silent grasses.

But before deciding that these novels are largely autobiographical, it is worth wondering about *Another Time, Another Place* as possibly a 'purer' work of fiction. Its themes and insights were surely reachable by a more detached narrator? For example, 'The Prisoners' is a wartime short story by Fred Urquhart that in many ways anticipates Kesson's themes here. [7] In it sympathy for the POW's loneliness and inability to communicate is mediated through the situation of Mary, a farmer's wife. In a very short space we see her complex feelings for her husband Will:

> After two years of marriage she was still in awe of her huge husband; more afraid of him than in love with him.

And like Kesson's young woman she is drawn to the Italians:

> Even in their captivity there was something romantic about them. They sang, and when they spoke of shouted to each other, their voices had a lilt. They brought an exotic note into the drab life of the farm. You felt that they should be going about with gold rings in their ears, that there should be bright sunshine and laughter and a ripe full moon and love.... She felt a fellow-feeling with them, she told herself. For after all, she was as much a prisoner as they were. A prisoner bound by her love and fear of Will.

She begins to talk with one Italian in a mongrel mixture of languages: he is anti-Fascist, he had to be 'taken' to the war, he never means to return to Italy. But when Will has to dispense with some workers he includes this one because he is not a good worker. The desolation of the POW who needs to communicate is balanced unobtrusively with that of the farmer's wife who has a desperate need for communication with her taciturn husband. So it is not necessary to trace too carefully the autobiographic elements in Kesson's tale: it is a perfect short study in loneliness and imprisonment, whichever way you look at it.

The young woman we meet at the start of the novella is only recently married: it still startles her to be addressed by her married name, 'Mistress Ainslie'. And we never learn her first name, a fact that emphasises her isolation. She has made a blind decision to marry an older man, a farm worker, with little idea of the life and circumstances this will involve, or the restrictive conventions of cottar living. This is stressed throughout, especially at the start. She recites a childish rhyme in her head that reflects her previous expectations:

> *If no-one ever marries me*
> *And I don't see why they should*
> *They say that I'm not pretty*
> *And I'm very seldom good* (p 1)

She is very young, and some of the children's songs that run through her head suggest she may have more in common with the farm children than the adults.

The opening of the novel is wet and windy, no use for harvest, and inimical to people. The driving rain blots out the surrounding country, and the Dornoch Firth – the story is set in a farm on the Black Isle, north of Inverness on the East of Scotland. But the places, like the protagonist, are not named: the isolation is complete. The weather seems hostile, and this recurs: the very words used here for gathering in the corn are repeated later:

> There would be no lifting of the tatties today, nor the morn,
> not if the rain kept dinging on like this. But the real storm,
> the furious conflict between the wind and the rain, was
> being waged high over the firth. (p 48)

No sooner have we been introduced to the unpleasant and tedious aspects of farm work which the young woman by her marriage has committed herself to, than Finlay, the farm foreman, arrives with startling news, that three Italian prisoners of war are coming to work on the farm. This, historically, was a widespread change: 'By July 1943, there were nearly forty thousand Italian prisoners at work in the fields, many of them billeted with farmers.' [8] For the young woman, this news is thrilling, a sign of all she has just begun to realise she is bound to miss because of her marriage:

> Prisoners-of-war, heroic men from far-flung places: the
> young woman felt a small surge of anticipation rising up

within her at the prospect of the widening of her narrow
insular world as a farm-worker's wife, almost untouched
by the world war that raged around her. She had always felt
she was missing out on some tremendous event, never more
so than when she caught a glimpse of girls of her own age,
resplendent in uniform, setting out for places she would
never set eyes on. Or when she caught their laughter-filled
whispers of a whirling social life, the like of which she had
never known. (p 3)

The other women react differently. Kirsty and Meg, the other two
wives in the three cottar houses, immediately worry about their pay-
packets, and whether this is a threat to them. It is different for the
crofter Elspeth. 'Of all their small community, Elspeth was the only
one involved in and affected by the war.' (p 5) She and her fiancé
Callum had meant to go to Canada after the war, but Callum was
reported missing at Monte Cassino and since that news there had been
no more talk of Canada. Elspeth withdrew from the farm rather than
have any dealings with the Italians. Elspeth and the young woman
were friends, and the young woman had shared Elspeth's dream of
Canada. But when Elspeth suggested she might one day visit, 'you've
got the whole world ahead of you yet', the young woman began to
realise what her marriage had meant:

She had thought that too. Before she was married. She had
thought she could go anywhere. Do everything... 'Not now
though Elspeth,' she had confided. 'It's all different now.
Being married, I mean...' (p 6)

In the end both women will be left stranded where they are, Elspeth by
her fiance's death in action, the young woman with all the monotony
of place, work and marriage, plus a Stand Still Order for farm
workers, and open shame for her husband and herself. Kirsty and
Meg will also remain where they are, but with no sign of reluctance.
They have both internalised the stifling conventions of life in this
hard place, and being inconspicuous is one of the chief. Kirsty will

not dance with the young woman at the harvest home dance, 'with everybody looking'. (p 40) The young woman reflects:

> *Nobody* was 'looking'. They should have gone through life invisible, Kirsty and Meg, their fear of attracting attention to themselves was so deeply rooted.
>   Even on social occasions like this, neither frill nor ribbon put forth a frivolous claim, no innocent coquetries, no small vanities. It was as if the whole chapter of their youth had been torn from their book, and they had turned the page from childhood to middle age. (pp 40-1)

Kirsty and Meg, although not belonging to the nearby village, insist on the young woman accompanying them to the flower show there:

> She *must* go, Kirsty insisted. They *always* went. It was expected. They all went together. The young woman would *have* to put in an appearance. Maybe, maybe she only imagined a tone of desperation in Kirsty's voice. A plea for reinforcement. (p 30)

The young woman is nearer in mind and spirit to the children, compared to birds.

So what do we learn of the young woman's husband, whose proposal had transformed her life so drastically? Not a great deal. We do not learn his name, or see his face. He is a good bit older, and taciturn. She has to adapt:

> Her man, she knew, wouldn't have very much to say about the Italians. Not in words. Always on his own, as a cattleman, and working apart from his fellow farm-workers, he had got out of the way of using words. Sometimes, sometimes she felt he had grown out of the need of words at all. She was learning though to interpret by look and mood. The way her man, himself, could interpret each need and nuance of the dumb beasts he worked amongst. (p 10)

He is obviously a decent and kindly man, but we never see him smile or hear him laugh. Indeed, there is not much laughter among any of the Scottish adults (except when we catch the young woman smiling at her reflection in the mirror). For the husband, the main event of the year, besides the birthing of the calves, is counting their hard earned savings, and deciding what to buy. The young woman in turn suggests new curtains, cockerels to rear for Christmas, bicycles, but he reasons against these and needs 'new planks to shore up the old hen-house' (p 67): nothing new or forward-looking, only vainly trying to mend the past. His sex-life is virtually unmentioned, but it is clearly unexciting: near the end the young woman remembers when the doctor thought she might be pregnant:

> She couldn't be pregnant, she had insisted. …She had tried
> to explain it to him. …Because. …You must *know*. When
> something important like that is happening.. You must
> know. You must feel something. I never feel anything. That,
> he assured her, was by no means uncommon. (p 93)

She has no awareness whatever of her sexual attractiveness until the advent of the Italians. Her efforts to impress Paolo in particular scandalise her neighbours. She has fondness and trust for her husband. When she falls romantically in love with Paolo, she is racked with guilt:

> The guilt she felt for the betrayal of her feelings towards her
> man. If he had been a bad man, she thought, as she watched
> him, quiet and serious, smoothing out the crumpled
> bank notes, or if only he had been her father, or even her
> brother… . (pp 66-7)

He might as well have been father or brother; in the marriage situation something important is clearly missing. Once, with near-simultaneous remorse, she imagines him lost in the war, and she realises how identical marriage and prison have become for her:

Dear God *forgive* me. The young woman was appalled by
the thought that had sprung so sudden and unbidden into
her mind. If her man had gone to the war and been killed,
she would have had a second chance. Another time to start a
new life, to be up and away from the ingrowing, incestuous
way of the farm, in search of something that had eluded her.
Often, in the evenings, when she stood watching the flow
of traffic far down on the main road and the smoke rising
up from trains rushing past on the other side of the firth, it
seemed as if a whole vista of escape unfolded itself before
her eyes.... . (p 97)

Eventually the young woman finds she cannot tell whether she is driven
to feel old beyond her time by the sheer monotony of the life, or by
the blind suddenness of her marriage: these become inseparable:

It was monotony that was beginning to make herself feel
old. Or maybe it was marriage that had shut a door, the
door that led to romance and adventure, one that she had
never given herself time to unlock. (p 84)

'I'm here forever', she thinks, feeling near despair. (p 102) Before she
eventually yields to Luigi's pleas, she sees her existence in the widest
possible perspective she can. Here she is forever an 'ootlin', in the
wrong time, the wrong place:

Times like these, the young woman felt imprisoned within
the circumference of a field. Trapped by the monotony of
work that wearied the body and dulled the mind. Rome
had been taken. The Allies had landed in Normandy, she'd
heard that on the wireless. 'News' that had caused great
excitement in the bothy, crowded with friends, gesticulating
in wild debate. Loud voices in dispute. Names falling
casually from their tongues, out of books from her school-
room days. The Alban Hills. The Tibrus.... . 'O Tibrus.
Father Tibrus. To whom the Romans pray'....Even in her

> schooldays, those names had sounded unreal. Outdistanced
> by centuries, from another time. Another place. The
> workers in the fields made no mention of such happenings.
> All their urgency was concentrated on reaching the end riggs
> at the top of the field. The long line of army jeeps roaring
> down along the main road provided nothing more than a
> moment for straightening their backs, never impinging on
> the consciousness of the turnip field. (pp 100-1)

The workers' minds come down, in all senses, to the turnip field.

The sudden arrival of three Italian prisoners of war, 'heroic men from far-flung places,' (p 3) has its seemingly inevitable effect on the young woman. She is ordered to have dealings with them; she is their caretaker and interpreter. She is fascinated by their very foreignness, by their colourful language, their emotional range, their physical embraces between men, their religion. Luigi from the first is the most blatant, and his first words to the young woman concern his poster Madonna before which he crosses himself devoutly, and the possibility that the young woman likes the 'jiggy-jig'. He evinces no understanding of the basic rule of nonfraternisation. He pursues her relentlessly, always with the same aim, and when any other young woman is seen, pursues her too. Where the young woman dreams of 'love' with Paolo, Luigi prosaically and urgently, wants sex. He is extravagant in all things, voluble, moody, querulous, questioning, egotistical.

> O, Luigi. A barrow-boy from the streets of Naples. She
> knew instinctively from memories of her own early street-
> spent, barefoot childhood, how it was for Luigi. Cocking a
> snook at the whole wide world. (p 19)

We never hear directly about any of their looks, but take it for granted that Paolo, who captures the young woman's attention, is the best-looking. He does not capture the reader's attention, however: in the whole novella he speaks only once, to complain that for all his complaints, Luigi is no sicker, no unhappier, than the other

two. Paolo is a handsome two-dimensional image in the novel, and
Umberto just the shadow of a shade.

The young woman in a new awareness of her body begins to dress
and do her hair to impress Paolo, and dreams that a week spent alone
with him would console her for a lifetime with her husband. But it
takes many vain attempts to catch his attention before she has to
accept that Paolo is not interested:

> It wasn't for Luigi that she had donned her short-sleeved
> blouse, or kilted her skirt up to her knees. And Paolo hadn't
> noticed. (p 23)

She is filled with dislike of Luigi at the harvest home: 'He wasn't
Paolo'. Gradually she realises that her feeling for Paolo is transparent,
that everyone but the man himself is aware of it. It is not until the
Italians' Christmas party that her new awareness of her sexuality is
fully manifested, when she dances at the centre of a band of admiring
Italians. She dances *with* Luigi, but *for* Paolo:

> '*Che bella cosa,*' he sang, his head thrown back, his eyes
> closed as they circled as if in a trance.
> '*Che bella cosa,*' the others took up the song, serenading
> her within a circle of music.
> '*Che bella cosa. . .*'
> Never before had she felt so desirable. Knowing in that
> moment how Eve must have felt, waking up from the trance
> of her creation, to look into the dark, appreciative eyes of
> Adam.
> Coyness, which until now, she hadn't known she possessed,
> took over. Brought to the surface by her awareness of
> Paolo's presence. Surely he would see her *now*, reflected in
> the admiration of other mens' eyes.
> Tomorrow, she would feel ashamed of her posturing,
> of her emphasis on her physical attributes. So blatantly
> displayed, an offering to Paolo. (p 78)

· Moments later, seeing him absorbed in conversation, unaware of her existence, she realises, 'It could never be Paolo.'

It is on this very night that Luigi begs yet again for 'jiggy-jig':

> For the first time, for seconds as long as centuries, she
> hesitated, trapped within her thoughts. She would lie quiet
> at nights now, by the side of her man, bereft of the ecstasy
> of her wakeful dreams, bereft of the possibility of Paolo.
> (p 79)

And now she makes her half-promise: 'Maybe...some day. One day.' After this half-promise, she enters a nightmare state, feeling trapped by it:

> She had felt safer when Paolo haunted her waking dreams
> than she felt now, confronted by the full-blooded reality of
> Luigi. (p 83)

A combination of circumstances leads to the apparently inevitable denouement. Else, the farmhouse servant, catches Luigi's eye – '*Ragazza...Che?*' (p 101) He goes off to learn more, leaving the young woman depressed by the word Luigi had earlier used only for herself. She feels herself getting older. '*Ragazza*. A title to which she felt she was losing her claim.' She realises,

> It was jealousy that ailed the young woman. Not of Else,
> herself, but of the single freedom Else enjoyed. Older than
> the young woman, Else was still '*ragazza*'.
> 'I'm here for ever,' she thought. (p 102)

Next time Luigi asks, she answers truthfully that she needs to do the milking, and he chases off after Else. A feeling of desperation takes her over, and when he asks again later, she pretends to have work to do:

It wasn't explanation enough. She knew that by the rigid
disbelief on Luigi's face. Turning away, she was unable to
look on him in the clear light of day, for she had raped his
privacy, had conjured up his every intimacy in fantasies
covered by the night. She felt the shame of it, tangible,
porous, oozing out to settle on her face. (p 109)

Quick to take advantage, Luigi urges her into the bothy. Afterwards,
she is filled with a storm of emotions, guilt, shame, a terror of
discovery, and a new kind of desire:

Her waking dreams of the night taking on confused
dimensions. Her body that had taken her unaware, asserting
a life of its own, clamouring for its needs, lay quiet now,
cold with apprehension. (p 110)

Now the structure of the novel takes a new turn, mirroring the
irreversible change that has happened to her. The last ten pages are
told in a patchy kind of retrospect, through her confused thoughts.
Suddenly the Italians have gone, and the young woman is climbing up
to Elspeth's croft to see whether, now they are gone, Elspeth will give
a hand with the stooking. The young woman briefly remembers the
departure, and her own immediate relief at the news. Luigi asked for
one last time, and confusedly she agreed. But everything has changed,
and she finds herself asking for what had never been offered:

The man who stood before her was no longer a prisoner.
No longer a servant of circumstances, as she herself
remained.... The triumph of this glistened on Luigi's face,
glinted in his eyes, as he leant forward to embrace her.... .
'Napoli. *Pronto*. Napoli.' The words, gasped in her ear,
were not intended for her hearing, but words of affirmation.
Of confirmation for himself. She was aware of that, as he
eased her down into the heather.
    In her fantasies of the night, consummation had been a
perfect thing, requiring no comment. Needing none of the

reassurance she heard herself beseeching now. 'ME *amo*, Luigi? ME *amo*...?
   '*Si, si. Ti amo.*'
'*Sempre,* Luigi. *Sempre.*'
'*Sempre. Si.*' (pp 115–6)

Her dignity gone, the young woman comes back to the news that Else has been assaulted in the wood. Suspicion immediately falls on Luigi. Now the awful ironies of the ending take shape. The young woman feels she must clear Luigi of the assault charge, no matter at what cost:

> But in the doing she was aware that her world as she now knew it would change, that the relationships she had begun to form would alter. She herself might survive the condemnation of the Cottar Row. It was the burden of shame within herself, and which would be extended to, and cast over her man, that was beyond enduring. (p 118)

They could move away? But she remembers the Stand Still Order, recently preventing farmworkers leaving the land. She remembers her interview with the officer who ignores her intention and says Luigi's misconduct with any civilian would convict him: he is bound for prison. All the young woman has left to hope for, as she reaches Elspeth's croft, is that Elspeth will break her silence, and if she's lucky, will renew her friendship: Elspeth asks her in, and renewed friendship is implied.

   It is easy in this desperate situation to make too much of the Italians' leaving present, a ship (imprisoned!) in a bottle, and a note giving her a name, Dina, and offering love and good wishes. There is surely a limit to the comfort that will offer, in the long years that lie ahead.

   This short novel is a marvel of economy and of delicacy of feeling. But it is of course mainly about the civilian young woman and her situation. The prisoners of war are crucial to the plot, and the ways in which they interact with the farmworkers tell us a lot about these civilians too. Douglas Gifford considers this novel 'the finest account of prisoners of war in Britain.'[9] But we don't hear much about the fighting: we never hear about the Italian soldiers' martial deeds or failures. Elspeth's fiancé is lost at Monte Cassino. But where did 'our' Italians fight? From all their confidences the young woman learns about their homes, their trades, their families, not their war experiences.

Essentially the book can be read as a fictional essay on the nature of imprisonment, but in a quite different way from the conventional novels about (usually) British POWS escaping from stalags. The civilians are prisoners too, know it or not. The young woman especially is herself a prisoner even as the Italians arrive. Her imprisonment is greatly intensified. The Italian prisoners lament, suffer, and then (except for Luigi) go home to get on with their lives. The young woman is 'here forever', with public knowledge of her guilty secret. Her husband will suffer too. How far can imprisonment go?

NOTES

1. The text quoted here is not the first edition, which was produced in haste to coincide with the advent of the Michael Radford film. All later editions have less cramped pages, a row of asterisks to indicate sections, and corrections to the phrases in Italian. They also suppress the misleading assertion on the blurb of the first edition that the young woman is a continuation of Janie from *The White Bird Passes*.

2. See Elaine Showalter, *The Female Malady: Women, Madness and English Culture 1830-1980*, London, 1987, *passim*.

3. See 'The Sma' Perfect: Jessie Kesson' in *Scottish Writers Talking 1*, ed, Isobel Murray, Kennedy and Boyd, Glasgow, 2008, p58.

4. See Isobel Murray, 'Jessie Kesson' in *A History of Scottish Women's Writing*, eds, Douglas Gifford and Dorothy McMillan, Edinburgh, 1997, *passim*, and Isobel Murray, '*The White*

Bird Passes: How Jessie Kesson Reached the Final Version', in *Scottish Studies Review*, Volume 7, No 1, Spring, 2006.

5.   See Linda Anderson, 'At the Threshold of the Self: Women and Autobiography' in *Women's Writing: A Challenge to Theory*, ed, Moira Menteith, Brighton, 1986, pp 54-71.

6.   See Isobel Murray, *Jessie Kesson: Writing Her Life*, second edition, Kennedy and Boyd, Glasgow, 2010, *passim*.

7.   'The Prisoners' was published in *The Year of the Short Corn*, 1949.

8.   Calder p 496.

9.   See Douglas Gifford, 'Literature and World War Two' in Ian Brown and Alan Riach, eds, *The Edinburgh Companion to Scottish Literature*, 2009, p 92.

STUART HOOD:
Carlino and A Den of Foxes

Dates: 1915–

Youth and Pre-War: Born and raised Edzell. English degree at University of Edinburgh. Teaching. Gifted in languages.

WW2: Italian East Africa and Middle East as infantry officer; then staff officer on operational Intelligence with Gordons. Captured North Africa; released from POW camp in Italy on Italians signing separate armistice: joined/led partisans. Service Holland and Rhine crossing with US 9th Army. Political Intelligence in Germany.

Novels: Carlino, 1963/1984; Since the Fall, 1955; The Upper Hand, 1987; A Den of Foxes, 1991.

Other war-related: Books on Fascism; the Holocaust; De Sade; International Socialism Journal, winter 2000, 'Memoir of the Italian Resistance'.

Post-War: Distinguished career in BBC: Controller of Programmes 1962–4; books on radio and television; Professor of Film, Royal College of Art.

Especially at the start, STUART HOOD's writing tended to give little away about the author. His first published work was *The Circle of the Minotaur* (1950), and it consisted of two short novels. The novella *The Circle of the Minotaur*, we are told on the dust jacket, is 'set in Italy after Mussolini's fall, after the Allies had advanced north of Florence.' Without this ephemeral explanatory note, it is quite hard to gather the context – names are in short supply; the story becomes almost fabular – and the novel does not deal with World War Two. We gradually learn that Carlo the protagonist left Italy to fight in the Spanish Civil War, and went on to fight as a partisan in France in World War Two. The novel is concerned with his return home to an Italian village some fifteen years after leaving, to the reputation of having murdered a prominent Fascist, although he did not do so. It is atmospheric, occasionally over-written, and laden with conflicting feelings of guilt over the death of a German boy Carlo did kill. *The Fisherman's Daughter* is even less specifically located. It is the tale of an escaped prisoner and his wanderings between prison and frontier in a strange country, with an inevitable (strange) meeting and a necessary death. Emotions of loneliness, fear, desire and anguish predominate. Learning later that the author was an Italian prisoner of war released – or deserted – by his captors in 1943 when they signed an armistice with the Allies will provide some sort of relieved sense of understanding to a confused but willing reader. And the same reader, if he or she perseveres, will recognise occasional incidents in the later memoir.

Hood's next treatment of his time in Italy during the war was radically different. *Pebbles from My Skull* (1963) was reissued and retitled *Carlino* with an Afterword in 1984 [cited as *Carlino* hereafter]. It is much more clearly and simply written, a personal memoir which engages the attention easily, and it comes as something of a surprise when the 1984 writer admits in his Afterword that the original contains 'something in the nature of a political vacuum.' [1] In the 1963 account Hood's precise political opinions – always a matter of great importance to the writer – have been quietly eliminated. From the start, then, the writer's political motivation, to fight against Fascism, is disguised, if only to protect his job – by 1963 the ex-Communist was an important executive with the BBC. But this does not appear a mutilated book. What *is* contained here is a clear, factual, honest-seeming and essentially personal account of the author's time in Italy, from the eighth of September 1943, when his Italian prison guards set free their four hundred Allied officer prisoners of war on their country signing a separate armistice with the Allies. Hood describes himself through various wanderings, fighting alongside partisans, hiding, even 'dawdling', daily waiting for the Allies to arrive, until the fifteenth of August 1944, when he was returned to England:

> Landfall with Blackpool tower just above the horizon. Four
> years before it had been my last sight of England. (p 129)

It is interesting to note that only these eleven months out of the four years service in what was called 'a good war' are treated here or elsewhere with any great depth. Before examining *Carlino* further, we must see that these eleven months constitute the irreducible hub of his experience, which he returns to again and again in his later work, usually fiction. From *Carlino* we learn virtually nothing of the experience of fighting and capture in North Africa, or the long days in confinement in Italy. What the prisoners all shared, says the author, is 'the traumatic shock of capture, the uneasy feeling that we should not be alive, the sense of failure'. (p 9) But that is all. In contrast, for one example, James Allan Ford fought as a young man in the brief farce of the battle for Hong Kong, and then endured years in a Japanese prison camp. Of the one he wrote an impressive battle-novel, *The Brave White Flag* (1961), and of the other a camp novel, *Season of Escape* (1963). But for Hood, the eleven months he spent in Italy and the experiences of that time stirred an itch that he has had to return again and again, to pick at, with insatiable curiosity about the Italian peasantry, the Italian partisans, the land, but most of all his personal experiences of close relationships with his peasant 'family', and his sometimes idiosyncratic feelings of guilt. It is certainly to my mind one of his best books.

As a memoir, *Carlino* is fresh, honest, moving. This reader noticed no political vacuum as the broadly Leftist hero moved through a complex series of emotional experiences. Hood was particularly well qualified for his particular adventure: a trained killer, he also spoke German, Italian and some Russian, all of which he had occasion to use; he had all the skills of an intelligence officer, and, perhaps under the circumstances best of all, 'I didn't look like an Englishman'. With his colleague Ted, the author wandered 'the wrong side of the Apeninnes, working in peasants' fields and stirred to 'a warm rush of political romanticism' at the word 'partisan' (p 32) But when joining the partisans becomes a possibility, difficulties arise. Whom do you trust, and what is he up to? This uncertainty is well conveyed. The partisans he contacts are a motley crew of deserters, immediately seen by the author as boys, who wait interminably for a possibility of action. Carlino wants them to post a night time guard, but is over-ruled. Then, in January 1944, Fascists attack the barn where the partisans are sheltering. A confused battle for the barn ensues, in which most of the partisans are killed. Should Carlino have insisted against opposition on posting a guard? He is haunted by such questions.

For a time Carlino is sheltered with a family in the middle of a village. There he endlessly reviews his part in the barn fiasco, and 'I was developing melancholia, sudden fits of black depression, such as I had not known since the worst days in prison camp – the kind of mood that made a man throw down his cards and leave the game without a word, to wrestle with himself in some sheltered corner, a blanket drawn over his face.' (p 73) Then a sudden Fascist intrusion into the village cancels all plans, and Carlino has to flee alone – with his school copy of Dante, an important literary companion. Despite peasant hospitality and kindness, the ensuing weeks are experienced as 'a nightmare of loneliness in which I began to lose my resolution and my very sense of direction.' (p 78)

'Thus aimlessly I drifted south through a moraine landscape and into Chianti'. (p 81) But now a healing experience follows, which is central to the whole book. Hood is admitted, even adopted, into a peasant family. Recovering, he locates all the ex-prisoners in the area, and tries to 'brace' them together. Knowing which of these to trust or rely on has not become any easier, but his acceptance by the peasant family and his confidence in the cause have a very positive effect:

> Chianti is the place where I passed some of the best months
> of my life…. . I had reached a point of equilibrium which
> allowed me to take each day as it came and look no further
> than the next. I was fitter than ever before in my life,
> covering such distances in a day that the peasants heard me
> with polite incredulity. I knew what I was doing. Was no
> longer alone. (p 100)

With a new sense of security, and as the Germans retreated, Hood
was able to 'wander' into Allied territory, where he was regarded
with suspicion. This account has been punctuated with more recent
news, from later visits to Italy, which question or verify relationships,
connections, but the original Epilogue asks the questions that seemed
most pressing at the time of writing, 1963, and they are big, self-
accusatory questions:

> Why did it take me from 8 September 1943 to 15 August
> 1944 to cross the line, reassume my identity, step back out
> of limbo?

He looks for honest answers:

> In part I was merely taking time out of life – escaping from
> war, which is itself an escape from reality…. . I had to escape
> from the reality of war into something more romantic.
> A fugue within a fugue…. . In the last analysis I dawdled
> because I liked it. There are moments in our lives when
> outward circumstances so exactly correspond to the inner
> structure of our being that our actions acquire an uncanny
> certainty. (p 131)

He had always been 'incredibly reserved', with few friends, most of
whom, because of the nature of his political beliefs, were virtually
fellow-conspirators. 'Yet there was nothing I wished more than to be
drawn intro a fuller community'. (p 132) In Italy, he had that happen, and
it is the openness of that account that makes the book memorable.

The 1984 Afterword looks back at the early work with the same searching honesty, but a change of focus. Hood's political reticence in 1963 is more than understandable: 'it would have been difficult for an executive of the BBC to admit that he had for some years been an active member of the young Communist League and then of the Party'. (p 141) This, even though he had allowed his Communist membership to lapse in 1945. His new perspectives on that time include finding that some of his 'memories' had been simply wrong, and finding other 'memories' now petrified into legend by the Italian Communist Party. He had also been rather dismayed by a sociological theory which down-valued human relationships, and suggested that an escaped prisoner was primarily simply an object 'of immense value' to Italian peasants. Nonetheless, Hood remained sure of the genuine human concern among his 'family' that had firmly marked the book. In the early Eighties he looked for and found many of these peasants again. Here is not the place to fill the political vacuum he found in the book, but it is the place for a humane endorsement:

> It leads me to reiterate what is I believe one of the most important discoveries I made during a time which was marked by many things that were difficult, frightening and painful: that in a world of cruelty and oppression there are still people who have generous impulses, courage and understanding. It is something that gives me, even in these dark and terrible times, when in so much of the world cruel and powerful forces have the ascendancy, a certain hope. It joins with the knowledge that in the most unexpected circumstances and at the most improbable conjunctures – for who would have thought that Mussolini's Italy, apparently so supine, would produce a resistance movement and a vast demonstration of political and human solidarity – the members of a society, of a class, undergo a transformation that endows them with courage and virtues beyond all possible expectation. (p 144)

He confirmed this to Bob Lumley in 1988. 'I found in a very important way I could rely on other human beings... . To put it crudely, it confirmed my faith in humanity.' [2] So *Carlino* is at bottom a very personal account of emotional experience in Italy during the war. But since leaving the BBC and other posts of responsibility, Hood has not been so reticent about his disillusionment with Russian Communism in 1945, and his search for a sound individual position. There are two main sources for the interested reader. The first, 'Memoir of the Italian Resistance', is an extremely clear and chronological account of the Italian resistance to Fascism which puts his own experiences recounted in *Carlino* into the context of the whole war in Italy. It shows that the very first Italian resistance groups began to form in November 1943, and Hood was already with *his* group that December. It also criticises the dismissive condescension of the Allies toward the Italians who opposed Fascism. This time he is writing for a chosen audience, the *International Socialism Journal*, in winter 2000. Interested readers are referred there. The other is an in depth personal interview he gave to Bob Lumley in 1988, in the *Edinburgh Review*, where he was asked and freely answered questions on a huge range of personal politics and emotions, and his subsequent careers in the media, as a translator, as professor. Interested readers ditto.[3] With either or both of these in mind, it is possible to read almost all Hood's fiction as having some bearing on the character or experience of 'Carlino', and to make almost certainly unwise identifications of some fictional characters as being partial portraits of the author. Hood has encouraged this kind of reading, for example with the suggestion to Lumley that the chief central characters of *The Upper Hand* are two different sides of his own character, but this ground is hardly safe. What we have to do now is to decide which of Hood's war-related novels after *Carlino* best deserves detailed treatment here.

(Of course, this is a very slanted way of approaching Hood's work. He is not just a war novelist, or even 'just' a novelist – although *A Storm from Paradise*, for example, won the Saltire Book of the Year Prize in 1985. His energy has produced output sufficient for several lifetimes.

He had an outstanding career in radio and television, becoming Controller of Programmes with the BBC in 1962, and made many fine film documentaries. He has written many non-fiction books, on Fascism; the Holocaust; the Marquis de Sade; on television. And he is a noted translator, of, for example, Riccardo Bacchelli, Dino Buzzati, Ciano, Ernst Junger and Pier Paolo Pasolini.)

But back to the 'war novels'. There are I think three possibles, with the third clearly ahead. But one fact is clear in all of them: since the careful 'peeling away of politics' that he achieved in *Carlino*, Hood has made it clear in writing about the war that his attitudes to that and to his political stance are inextricably linked. The first of these is *Since the Fall*, a novel of 1955. This concerns the adventures in Italy of a number of ex-inmates of 'Camp 50' in a post-war organisation something like UNESCO. The sympathetic character, Gavin Hamilton, is the victim of a Calvinist conscience which will prevent his success in this world. Choice of names is interesting here. We remember Burns's 'Holy Willie's Prayer, where the hypocritical Elder accuses and prays against Gavin Hamilton, and the 'Argument' points out that Hamilton is 'one of the most irreproachable and truly respectable characters in the country.' (Robin Jenkins would use the same name ironically in *A Would-Be Saint* (1979) and *The Pearl-fishers* (2007).) *Since the Fall* is set up as a farce, with a comic Basil Seal-like antihero with no scruples who makes himself a lucrative corner in air-ballooning Western propaganda into Eastern Europe, casually betrays Gavin with a 'Poor Gavin' aside, and is destined for great things, while Gavin, like Tony Last in *A Handful of Dust*, goes, having lost his love, into a foreign unknown, in this case a Presbyterian Guinea, to expire there. I'm suggesting a considerable comic gift here, which is less apparent elsewhere, and I think the novel's disappearance from the communal consciousness is a pity, but the amount of attention paid to the war itself does not make it fit for purpose here.

The second novel in which the war is inescapable – but again secondary – is *The Upper Hand* (1987). Here the reader of the rest of Hood's corpus of fiction and prose is at a certain advantage: certain preoccupations emerge again, and certain experiences are economically re-used. Not only that, but the author's personal experiences seem to be parcelled out between the two main characters. He told Lumley that the experience of writing it was therapeutic, and the book comes after he underwent psychoanalysis:

> One of the characters is a documentary producer dealing
> in a high culture area, who has been a member of the
> Communist party. The other character is a sort of radio
> hack at Bush House, and he is a member of MI5. (p 204)

Colin Elphinstone is the ex-Communist, charming, charismatic and talented, and his friend (or antagonist) is the narrator, John Melville, who never comes to terms with his fascination, envy, perhaps hatred of the other. While Colin had a 'good war', John was engaged in 'the book-keeping of war' (p 43) in intelligence: Hood of course covered both. This may, as Hood hinted, be a classic treatment of the 'divided self', so dear to Scottish tradition.

> I had none of Colin's romantic notions, no passionate
> commitment to equal Greenspan's, none of the drive and
> courage of the tunnellers up there in Berlin – only a deep
> scepticism about human motives and a pervading distrust of
> enthusiasm. (p 136)

In contrast, Colin's final raki-soaked monologue gives a romantic version of the thinking of the author himself:

> I once was hooked on a millennium and still cling – against
> all the evidence – to a vestigial hope that, perhaps, out of
> the blood and suffering and shit and in spite of the lies, the
> killings, the mockeries of justice committed in the name of
> Communism, a seed of hope will one day spring somewhere
> on this benighted planet, maybe even in the East, and that
> we shall see not the millennium, but a prospect of a new
> and better society. (p 180)

The struggle between the two is convincing, perhaps because John is such a cold and rather mean character, but many other characters in the book fail to come alive, and are barely distinguishable. The war is over in fifty pages, but the emphasis, the climax, is much later, when John betrays Colin as consciously as Peter did Gavin in *Since the Fall*.

A Den of Foxes (1991) is not 'just' a war novel: it is a book which by complex intercutting and interpolation attempts to bring together and make sense – or patterns – out of its protagonist's whole adult life, including the decisive wartime experiences. In it, Peter Sinclair is brought face to face by indirection, with the experiences and the political choices that have informed the kaleidoscope of his life. It is not for nothing that Stuart Hood spent time translating contemporary continental masters of post modern techniques: *A Den of Foxes* shows their influence, and requires a patient and careful reader, who will no doubt want to start again after that first careful reading.

Peter Sinclair is an ageing academic with a secret fear that he is already marked by the approach of death in a mole-like appearance gradually increasing on his chest. He has left his job, ostensibly to write a book, and has retreated to a small cottage in Scotland 'to take stock of his life' (jacket) and to come to terms with the prospect of mortality. He is willingly diverted by a letter from Italy, from an Englishman living where the bulk of Sinclair's war experience was gained, La Volpaia in Tuscany. Christopher Williams ('Urizen') has invited him to start an intriguing venture, war-gaming. Peter has hardly consented and been invited to supply the details of his PC (Principal Character), when a narrator breaks in, addressing the reader:

> I have generated the following character for you as readers: Your PC is called Peter Sinclair. He is... (p 9)

Effectively the reader has been made a participant in a war-game, and is now told the relevant facts about Sinclair himself – sixty-four, a 'good war', married twice, 'a person of the Left...politically unattached', an ex-Communist. Thus in a few pages the reader is participant or observer in two war-games and already warned of Sinclair's war, he will soon be:

> On the move once more, as if trying to shake off a pursuer.
> Perhaps even to San Vito which he had known when
> engaged in other, grimmer wargames. (p 8)

Nothing proceeds to get simpler. Soon we are involved in a multiplicity of narratives; letters between 'Urizen' and Peter on the progress of the wargame on planet Andromeda; and Peter's Scottish adventures, where in particular he encounters the estate-owner's niece Lucy, a beautiful and independent young woman on a motor cycle who comes and goes at will, and a former student, Duncan Hogg, a Marxist autodidact who despises Peter's lack of political commitment. Peter gradually tires of the wargame, but he begins to be involved in the life situations and choices of the main characters he has invented on Andromeda in 2087. These are significantly and rather ironically named David Balfour and Catriona, as in Stevenson, with David the focus, conventional, moral and safe, while Peter's Catriona, unlike Stevenson's, is her own woman, secretly reacting against the oppressive rule of the colony, and holding on to some kind of dream of a millenarian future. Peter is moved to write a scenario explaining the evolution of Andromeda, and then a lengthy 'Prognostication' of what earth would be like in 2087. (pp 50-56) But these documents are not of course presented together or sequentially; the narrative is much more clipped and apparently disconnected than that.

It is frequently interrupted, for example, by reference to Vladimir Propp, the Russian theorist of the morphology of folk tales. The anonymous narrator attempts from time to time to approximate Peter's story to Propp's theory, and identifies various parallels or possibilities, with indifferent success.

There are also times when Peter is faced with memories of his past, like his love for his second wife Orna, an anti-Zionist Israeli who eventually left Peter, discontented with his fastidious dithering over joining any political organisation whatever. She left him, taking their young son Yoram, who must now be old enough for military service in Israel. Again, after Orna there was Anna, a married librarian with whom Peter had a protracted secret affair before he took early retirement.

At another point, Peter is writing a wargame for David Balfour on Andromeda, and is reminded of a piece of his own war, when the Germans were in retreat on the Dutch border, and he, like Hood, was a staff officer after his wound in Italy and working in Intelligence predicting troop movements, but can only watch the entrapment of Allied troops:

> But Peter carried with him the memory of a boy at a
> forward aid post weeping, calling on his mother as he
> watched the blood pump from his shattered leg and knew he
> was going to die. (p 61)

This kind of haunted, guilty memory is typical of sympathetic characters from Hood's earlier books also.

The reliving of Peter's war time in Italy is recorded in snatches, often inspired by what he is writing about the doings of David Balfour on Andromeda. Peter was dropped into Tuscany with four Italian companions from Bari, where he has been trained as a saboteur. He realises near La Volpaia that he is about to draw the whole landscape and people into 'a wargame plotted hundreds of miles away'. (p 115) He sees 'the aerial assembly of the radio station and signals centre it was his mission to destroy'. He meets Italian partisans, men 'who felt that something must be done if they were to look each other in the eye when they were free men once more'. (p 117) Peter's orders are to destroy the radio station, and to harass German convoys. Dario warns of inevitable reprisals against civilians, but Peter sticks to his orders. By the time of liberation four weeks later, Peter is the only survivor of a group of three. A little later we are to share his memories of the reprisals too, and he will be haunted by his memories, however briefly reported: while his men can lie up in the safety of the woods and plan their next action:

But when the punitive column arrived about midday few of the peasants in the hillside farms had time to flee. They died with their wives and children and their white oxen in the burning ruins of their homes. (pp 125–6)

Meanwhile, back in the present in Scotland, Peter resigns from the wargame, but continues to write about and becomes obsessed by his two space-scout characters, David Balfour and Catriona. It all becomes even more complex when David takes part in wargaming on Andromeda, and his co-ordinator is a member of the powerful authority, called Peter Sinclair! He turns out to be reputedly the grandson of the man of the same name who first came to the planet from Earth (Tellus) with the first settlers, and to be the same Peter Sinclair whose story we are following in 1987. This man encourages David in the replay as wargame of our Peter's actual observed battle on the Dutch/German border late on in the war. But he has a more sinister side. When another party from Tellus arrives on Andromeda, the authorities brand them not as strangers but as intruders, and Catriona's first overt sign of rebellion is to refer to them as strangers, simply. The Andromeda Peter Sinclair debriefs them separately, and clears David of fault but re-interviews Catriona. Eventually he gives her his grandfather's record to read, *An Apology for My Life and Beliefs by Peter Sinclair: 1987*. Catriona finds the account of our Peter's generation and his political opinions on earth difficult, and in places impossible, but some extracts strike a chord:

I belong to that generation which grew up in the aftermath of one great war. We were convinced that another must come soon and that it would involve us. From this it followed that one strong impetus – not the only one but a determining one – behind our political commitment was a desire to fight for peace, against war, against the merchants of death and their clients, the Fascist states.

It was our determination to fight Fascism, together with our perception of the social injustices of capitalism – poverty alongside wealth, scarcity alongside profusion, the

oppression of the colonial peoples, the exploitation of men
and women for profit – that made us give our allegiance
to the Party which seemed to make our causes its own: *the*
Party. (p 171)

She finds Peter's account of his 'mental and moral struggles' as he
learns more of Stalin's tyrannies 'difficult', but is impressed by the
way he holds on to 'a dream of something':

What that dream appeared to be was a just society in which
the great wealth of the earth was distributed equitably
among its inhabitants and the exploitation of men and
women by others, of one race by another, of one sex by
another, would at last – at some perhaps distant date – be
banished from the earth. (p 173)

This dream, 'the old heretical dream of a good society', links Hood
back to Naomi Mitchison. When her African novel *When We
Become Men* was published in 1955, an anonymous blurb-writer
wrote: 'Naomi Mitchison read Plato's *Republic* when she was fifteen
and ever since she has been looking for the just society.' Not for
either writer to be found in Plato, but 'a dream of something' to be
constructed in the future.

But Catriona is also impressed by 'the writer's pessimism' (p
175): the end of the *Apology*, as she reads it, is, 'It will be another
generation at least before it will be possible to discuss seriously and
hopefully humanity's dream of something'. (p 176) But *her* Peter
Sinclair on Andromeda insists that:

What I would assert is a law of nature is that the dreamers
of such utopias end up as fanatics, killing and oppressing
others in the name of justice, peace and love. (p 181)

In the first ending *our* Peter Sinclair writes for David and Catriona,
she persists in greeting the 'strangers', and David is ordered to follow
and fire on her, which he does.

Back in 1987 Peter is officially invited back to Tuscany for a ceremony to commemorate the liberation of the town of San Vito, 'to which he had in no small measure contributed'. (p 113) But when he attends he feels 'drawn into the rhetoric of celebration': 'he was being, he felt, inserted in a legend which he could not decently disavow for it was charged with too much emotion, too much genuine feeling, too much political nostalgia.' (p 124) The Italian Communist Party has set it all in the stone of legend, and Peter feels, significantly, like 'an alien intruder'. (p 131)

Having gone so near to La Volpaia, he dares himself to go there, the den of foxes. Here, directly or indirectly, he encounters a deal of his past. Staying with Urizen the wargamer, he meets urbane Zionist Peled, an Israeli who knew Peter's ex-wife Orna, now, he says, part of 'the loony Left'. (p 132) Peter remembers Orna's warnings against Peled, who may be part of the powerful secret Israeli Mossad. He also finds his ex-mistress Anna along with her husband; he meets Duncan Hogg, his former student, who has faked a reference from Peter to get a job with Urizen. And he hopes ardently to meet Lucy again, whom he now identifies in his mind with Andromeda's Catriona. Duncan has told him Lucy is faithful, in her fashion, to a Palestinian boyfriend who has been in an Israeli jail for the last two years.

When she does arrive, Peter realises that he can never occupy the space in her life that she does in his. He is always haunted by fear of disease and death, and the unnecessary deaths of the past:

> He thought uneasily of the peasants murdered in their steadings and of other killings; like that of a German straggler, looking for eggs or milk maybe, whom they had surprised sitting beside a path through the vines. When he made a move to get his rifle Aldo had slashed his throat with his pennato. The body was there somewhere among the high broom on the slope beyond La Volpaia. (p 130)

Duncan rebukes him for his wargaming:

> 'It's fucking pathetic. You and your generation refighting
> your bloody stupid battles. You'd think you'd have got over
> it by now.'
> 'I'm not sure,' said Peter, 'that it's something one can ever
> get over.'(p 153)

Peter's last dealings with Lucy provoke a blind mission in a martial cause. They involve a chaste closeness and intimacy. She is on a mission that she does not pretend to explain, but he obeys her in blind trust. She wants him to photograph a yacht Peled has been visiting. Without hesitation or explanation Peter goes and does what she asks, just before the social party at La Volpaia breaks up after a row between Peled and Duncan over the Holocaust and Zionism. It is only after Peter has settled back in his Scottish cottage that he hears on the radio of 'a terrorist attack on an Israeli yacht' in which Peled has been killed. At last he makes an appointment to see the consultant whose bad news he has feared all along, and he writes two more things. First, he adds a paragraph to the *Apology* that Catriona read on Andromeda, pointing to humanity's embracing 'the old, heretical dream of a good society'. (p 212) Then he writes a new ending to the story of David and Catriona, one in which David does not destroy her, and in which she greets the 'intruders' as 'sisters and brothers'.

Perhaps only by such a convoluted story-telling could an unsentimental journey such as Peter's be conveyed. Peter learns again as an older man the ability to pursue action for an idea which he saw over simply before he met the realities of war, and performs an act of unselfish love, knowing he is not to profit from it. The novel ends with the admission from the anonymous narrator:

> I cannot find in Propp anything that casts light on the
> human condition. (p 217)

NOTES

1. *Carlino*, Manchester, 1985, p 140.

2. 'Keeping Faith: An interview with Stuart Hood' by Bob Lumley, *Edinburgh Review* 79-80, 1988, pp 172-206, p 184.

3. Lumley, pp 172-206.

George Mackay Brown
and *Beside the Ocean of Time*

Dates: 1921–96.

Youth and Pre-War: Born and raised in Stromness, Orkney.

WW2: Called up, but rejected as unfit: tuberculosis. Spent the war as a civilian in Orkney.

Novels: *Greenvoe*, 1972; *Magnus*, 1973; *Beside the Ocean of Time*, 1994.

Other war-related: Autobiography, *For the Islands I Sing*, 1997.

Post-War career: Edinburgh University 1956–60, English: 1960–2 Research on GM Hopkins. Writer in Orkney.

GEORGE MACKAY BROWN was called up to serve in the Second World War, but was found unfit to serve: the diagnosis was tuberculosis. Nonetheless the war was a huge part of his life experience in Orkney, and made a huge impact on his imagination, and consideration of war in general is certainly essential to a measured view of his work. The trouble in the present context is, that his imagination so often went beyond the Second World War, and indeed into a future too awful for many of us to contemplate.

Poet, story-teller, novelist and dramatist, George Mackay Brown is unique among the writers surveyed here, in many ways. He was born in 1921 and raised in Orkney, and rarely travelled beyond it. The island world he knew as he grew up was a quiet, traditional one, with farmers and fishermen and small shopkeepers, plus a few doctors, lawyers and teachers, and – way at a distance – the landowners, occasional visitors, with loud English voices that astonished the natives. When the Second World War threatened, he and his brothers 'thought it would be a great adventure too – going to the war'.[1] Three brothers did go (and returned safely), but Mackay Brown soon succumbed to his first bout of TB and remained at home, an unfit civilian. This did not of course mean simply remaining in his pastoral island tranquillity. The war came to Orkney with a vengeance: the Fleet came to Scapa Flow, there were soldiers guarding it, a Navy base at Lyness, wartime airbases for fighters. So his early near-paradisal notion of Orkney was spoiled:

> The Second World War brought more huge transfusions of money and people. This time soldiers predominated; they ringed Scapa Flow with such a density that the German bombers, after one or two forays early in the war, never came back. Servicemen of many countries were stationed in Orkney. [2]

His biographer Maggie Fergusson describes it:

> Orkney underwent an invasion of troops. Shipload after shipload descended the gangplank of the tubby troopship

the *Earl of Zetland*, until in the end 60,000 servicemen
and women had arrived in the islands: three to every
native Orcadian... . Nissen-hut villages sprang up like
mushrooms around Scapa Flow. Road-blocks, pillboxes
and anti-tank traps were set up on all the approach
roads to Stromness, and between them snaked cordons
of barbed-wire entanglements, so that the town was
completely encircled against invasion.[3]

This influx and all the activity made a sad change for Mackay
Brown. The invasion was to him intensely destructive, and it figures
at length in both his first novel, *Greenvoe* (1972) and his last, *Beside
the Ocean of Time* (1994). It was surely no accident that when Bob
Tait and I interviewed him at length in 1984 he said that he mainly
wrote about an 'Orkney of fifty years ago', and used this 'to remind
people of the essential first things and the four elements and that'.
(SWT 1 p 43) Everything he wrote centred on Orkney, its history, its
farms, its ways of life and its people, always including the drunks,
the tinkers and the beachcombers, and the work is usually, as he
said, set some decades ago.

His imagination is possessed by natural and supernatural rhythms,
the rhythm of the seasons, of man's life from birth to death, of
ploughing, sowing, reaping and harvest, with another rhythm of
divine protection and care, often expressed in the language of the
rituals and ceremonies of the Roman Catholic church, which Mackay
Brown joined as a mature adult in 1961. His work in every genre is
suffused with coalescing images: images from his day to day pre-war
Orkney experience, fishermen with ploughs, simple pastoral images
of silver fish and green or golden cornstalk, and images from the
New Testament where Jesus called fishermen to become 'fishers of
men', performed miracles with loaves and fishes, and told parables
in simple country language: 'A sower went forth to sow...'; 'Except
a corn of wheat fall into the ground and die...'. And also images
of Christ's life and death rendered through Catholic devotional
tradition, the joyful, sorrowful or glorious mysteries of the rosary,
the Stations of the Cross and the Passion, and the sacraments. His

Christianity is essentially sacramental. This is the basic source of the pictures of Orkney we find in his work.

But an undercurrent in his work about modern Orkney is always one of lamentation at modern change, which he sees as impoverishing the community, and at the gradual disappearance of the communities themselves – something either begun or greatly accelerated by the wartime defences on Orkney. The war passed, of course, but it had an indelible impact on Mackay Brown, for whom just the names of battles or atrocities were sufficiently moving. But his writing life coincides more with the Cold War that followed, and for him the threat of nuclear destruction overrode everything – what he calls in *An Orkney Tapestry* (1969) 'the atom-and-planet horror at the heart of our civilisation' or 'a Black Pentecost'. In the poem sequence *Fishermen With Ploughs* (1974), it is 'the Dragon, black pentecostal fire'. The possibility of nuclear war, of mankind's simultaneous self-destruction and the destruction of all creation, is a horrifying constant threat, and often subsumes all his other ideas of war. This is what gives potency to the evil image at the heart of his first novel *Greenvoe* (1972), the Black Star. The Black Star is a negation of all the stars in our experience, and clearly some ominous, war-and-nuclear-related new installation. In *Ten Modern Scottish Novels* (1984) Bob Tait and I tried to understand the nature of the threat as the author saw it:

> Christ as man accepts death, and conquers death, and in his resurrection the resurrection of all men is made possible. Mackay Brown's powerful vision here is of a different Incarnation, an evil or black one. Satan enters the world of time and Greenvoe as a Black Star, a hideous, death-dealing parody of the liberating, life-bringing Christ. The Black Star then withers, destroys, freezes, produces an apparently final negation. Of course the very word Incarnation is inappropriate here: Christ was 'made flesh', but the Evil that enters Hellya with Black Star is so anti-human that it takes the form of inanimate modern building materials, especially the concrete Mackay Brown so much deplores. [4]

But the islanders have no idea of what is happening:

> What exactly was happening up there between the Glebe
> and Korsfea? It was impossible for any villager or islander
> to find out – the almost completed fence was too well
> guarded by men and dogs and barbed wire – but it seemed,
> from things the labourers said in drink, that a system of
> tunnels was being dug into the heart of the island, five
> of them in all (said Jock MacIntosh the foreman from
> Glasgow) radiating out from one central underground
> chamber. So it was indeed a kind of black star that was
> being burned and blasted under the roots of Korsfea and
> Ernefea and The Knap.... It could be some kind of atomic
> work, they could not say.... Greenvoe shrivelled slowly in
> the radiance of Black Star. (pp 215–7)

While the soulless but realistic invasion of Greenvoe by faceless
bureaucrats and builders and tunnellers is horrible, it is dwarfed by the
menace of Black Star. As the novelist has it in his autobiography:

> Of course Orkney had, twice in the early part of the twentieth
> century, experienced vast irruptions into its pastoral life-cycle
> – the outpouring of troops and ships in the two world wars;
> populations here and there had creaked and cracked under
> the pressure. A few merchants had prospered well: torrents
> of gold poured through their tills. Farmers had had to leave
> their ancestral fields at short notice to make way for military
> emplacements and runways. Young Orkney men sailed away
> to their death in France or in the air or in Atlantic convoys.
> But those incursions lasted for only a year or two; the tide
> ebbed, leaving ugly concrete scabs here and there that had
> been campsites and gun-and-searchlight emplacements; and a
> high-water fringe of money where the flood had lapped.
>   It was something vaguely like this – preparations for a third
> world war, much more hideous than its two predecessors –
> that I imagined as the destroyer of the village and the island. [5]

For this, the whole village of Greenvoe – indeed the whole island of Hellya – is cleared of its inhabitants, even those whose families have farmed there for a thousand years. The theme of clearance is a potent one in modern Scottish fiction, and here includes a shiftless population of drifters and dependents, as well as minor business people, who are portrayed as living somewhat in the past when the novel begins, with, for example, itinerant Indian pedlars coming over each year to supplement the meagre contents of Mrs Olive Evie's shop.

Greenvoe takes place over a symbolic 'week', which renders the community fairly fully, and then destroys it. But it establishes narrative patterns and features of a kind the author would make again. For example, the narrative is punctuated by snatches of the slanted version of local history recounted in the pub by The Skarf, a fisherman with Communist leanings – and, we later learn, incipient multiple sclerosis. On each 'day' of the narrative, we are treated to one of his narratives, and each 'day' is rounded off by mysterious figures performing The Ancient Mystery of the Horsemen, which at the end offers a far-off hope for the island. Mackay Brown was very conscious of these patternings: in 1984 he admitted serenely to us; 'that's an old trick of mine, of course, that's what happens in *Time in a Red Coat* too. And lots of stories and that with that sort of development'.[6] This is only one of the many 'tricks' the first-time novelist used, to combat any illusion of simple realism or straightforward linear time, with different linguistic styles alternating, and marvellously telling short conversations between the islanders.

Greenvoe is an astonishing first novel, which Bob Tait and I have claimed achieves the loving creation of an imperfect, often comic community, with remarkable, almost reckless virtuoso modulations of style: but its destruction, with science overcoming humanity in the installation of Black Star and the clearance of the people, is horribly conveyed.[7] Similarly *Fishermen With Ploughs* (1974) is a poem cycle about an attempt to re-establish an agricultural community after the devastation of a nuclear war, with very limited success – and a less optimistic conclusion than *Greenvoe*. *Greenvoe* ends with a hope of a distant future 'resurrection' for the island, much as Mitchison's poem 'Clemency Ealasaid' offers a far distant forgiveness and renewal long after the war. We discussed this overhanging threat with Mackay Brown in 1984, interestingly without any of us actually specifying it:

> **IM** For a writer who is not in any obvious way politically committed, you've actually written *more* about that particular subject than most contemporary writers have.
>
> **GMB** It's such a fearful thing.
>
> **IM** And you've actually faced in *Fishermen With Ploughs* in particular, the concept of the whole thing happening. ... *Fishermen With Ploughs* is a very much more ambivalent and grey thing.
>
> **GMB** Dark grey.
>
> **IM** On the whole you don't write about contemporary subjects, but that is *one* that you come back to.
>
> **GMB** That's the one that overshadows everything, I think. [8]

This indicates clearly enough that it was the threat of 'mutually assured destruction' that pre-occupied Mackay Brown in these works. But his second novel, *Magnus* (1973), went back to his major historical interest in Orkney and the Vikings of the sagas: it is certainly not a novel of the Second World War! St Magnus was an important figure for the author, who returned to him in several genres.[9] The basic situation involves a time when the intricacies of descent left two earls, Hakon and Magnus, as rightful rulers. Briefly, almost all realised this could not work; the islands needed a single ruler. Hakon and his men decided on Magnus' death: he made alternative suggestions of pilgrimage and exile, the religious life, even mutilation and imprisonment, but then accepted the inevitable with saintly calm, freely forgiving his executioner. It is easy to argue, as some have, that the novel is in places overwhelmed with spiritual meditation and biblical images, dreams of wedding garments and man's religious development from human sacrifice to the self-sacrifice of Christ, but what most early reviewers naturally seized on was the treatment of Magnus' death.

This is because the actual execution of Magnus in the twelfth century is suddenly switched to the execution of Lutheran pastor Dietrich Bonhoeffer in a concentration camp during the Second World War. Mackay Brown writes in his autobiography that incidents such as the death of Magnus 'are repetitions of some archetypal pattern':

> The life and death of Magnus must therefore be shown to be contemporary, and to have a resonance in the twentieth century. I did not have far to go to find a parallel: a concentration camp in central Europe in the spring of 1944.
>
> Magnus appears as Pastor Bonhoeffer (or another like him) and is executed in circumstances and by people compared to whom the twelfth-century Norse killers perform with a ritualistic inevitability: there is a kind of tragic beauty, even, in what they do, far removed from the hideous slaughter-houses of the Nazis. (p 179)

But although I think *Magnus* is Mackay Brown's least successful novel, I don't think this sudden move into the twentieth century is the reason: I outlined my reasons above. I think the modern reader could take the timeshift in his stride. The reason for the comparative failure of *Magnus* is, for me, the loss of grip on narrative, in the whole section of the novel called 'The Killing', which occupies almost half the book. If we look at that section in any detail, what makes it falter is too much reflection and philosophising, in a totally non-narrative mode, and over-detailed rendering of the long conversation between Hakon's drunken men and Magnus' men the night before, or the other modern importation, an episode of docudrama where individual islanders show a general unwillingness to be involved in any way in the dire doings on Egilsay that Easter. The reflections are on the changing evolution of sacrifice through the ages, with the coming of Christ at last: 'That was the one only central sacrifice of history.' (p 158) And there is a detailed but oddly distanced account of Magnus' thoughts during the last Mass before his death. After all that, the German chef's first-hand account of being picked out as an executioner is a relief. Livolf was chef only to the camp's administrators. He stresses that he lived outside the camp, and protests that the stench of the new ovens in the camp and especially the venture of killing the prisoner had nothing to do with him. The scene actually becomes more vivid, as Hakon is transformed into a troubled camp commandant and his followers into drunken SS officers, and it ceases abruptly when Livolf cannot remember anything of the prisoner's actual death.

The subject of Mackay Brown's third novel, *Time in a Red Coat* (1984), is war itself, throughout time, and its main method is poetic and symbolic rather than realistic:

> Well, the theme of it is war, and it's treated in rather a strange way, because there's this girl who was born in China, somewhere vaguely in the East, you know, and she was born during the beginning of a war after maybe hundreds of years of peace. And this same girl, she wanders through history for about two thousand years maybe, and gradually comes westwards through Asia and Russia and into Germany and all different parts of Europe about the time of Napoleon; and finally – she never seems to age very much – maybe just a year or two and finally, she comes to Orkney in the last two chapters, and that's about the basic thing… she can see into the future; into the wars to come – which God forbid, because I don't think many of us will be alive to tell about it.[10]

So she visits real-and-symbolically-universal places, the Well, The Inn, The Battle, and so on. Each war in history is part of 'the Dragon'.

No more than *Magnus* is this a novel about the Second World War, but that war figures in it briefly but very powerfully. It seems to me a much more successful novel, with Mackay Brown's narrative imagination creating powerful images and sketches in each chapter, giving it a sense of movement. Toward the end the girl visits a nineteenth-century 'Magus' who not only has a vast museum of all the wars that have left traces, but can actually grant access to future records. The girl sees it all - here, the wars of the twentieth century:

She looked at a wooden cross with a number on it; a
poster with a cold eye and finger aimed out of it; YOUR
COUNTRY NEEDS YOU; a rag tangled in a length of
barbed wire; a lampshade made of the tattooed skin of a
man; a stone that had a shadow burned on it by such pure
close intensity of heat that the sun, in comparison, is a
feeble candle; a gas mask; seven rats' skeletons, with teeth
marks, and even an incision to show that in some cellar
a human being had feasted on them; an arm-band with a
swastika; drawing-board sketches of such future weaponry
as the submarine, the tank, the entire rocket family from the
V-1 on to the air-to-air missile; a skull that had a shell and
drifted crystals of salt in its chambers – a sailor's; seven tin
helmets, of different designs, one dented, one with a bullet-
hole clean through it; a cluster of incendiary bomb-fins that
must have made a merry little fire in some vennel; a crust of
grey bread from some place called Stalingrad... .
In the last case lay a lump of uranium ore. (pp 214-5)

This could include a neighbour's friendly mention of the tin hat that
saved Linklater's life. But at the end is the 'lump of uranium ore.'
And during the ending of the novel, relatively happy and pastoral,
comes a report of 'men coming at the weekend to make probes into
the hill... . What the samples are for, I don't know.' (p 244) And
only weeks before the publication of *Time in a Red Coat* the author
said in our interview: 'There's deposits of uranium, you know, just
round Stromness mainly, and they might open a mine there any time,
I suppose, if they want to'.[11]

So World War Two is only a relatively small part of this book, but
the treatment is telling. The girl sees moving images on the screen:

The first mutterings then of the Second World War, truly
so called, because hardly an individual on the globe wasn't
influenced by those horrendous festivals of fire and blood.
    Italian armies overran Abyssinia, so that the bull-frog
dictator of Italy could add the empty title 'Emperor of

Ethiopia' to the impotent royal house in Rome, and distract an impoverished badly-ruled people with a poor dream of glory. Reactionary professional armies in Spain destroyed protractedly over three years amateur armies of socialists, anarchists, idealists and 'progressives'. First bombs were dropped on an open city: Guernica. These dreadful scenes were but a prologue.

I need but name places: names will suffice. Warsaw, Sedan, Dunkirk, Narvik – Minsk, Smolensk, Leningrad, Moscow, Stalingrad – Pearl Harbour, Singapore – the North Atlantic convoys and the iron sharks that preyed on them – London, Coventry, Hamburg, Dresden – the long battle for the Pacific islands – Berlin, Hiroshima, Nagasaki. (p 224)

The last thing she sees of the war is the destruction of the Jews. 'All the dogs of Europe became rabid in the first half of the twentieth century'. But again, he does it all with a short, intensely evocative list: 'I will mention names: Dachau, Auschwitz, Treblinka, Babi Yar.' (p 225)

It might indeed seem that Mackay Brown had said all he needed to about this war by now, but he was to write another novel, involving a contemporary caught up in it. Oddly, though, *Beside the Ocean of Time* (1994) is not much focussed on the horrors of its central character being a prisoner of the Nazis: rather, it does leave a lasting impression of the way the war indirectly devastated the fictional small island of Norday.

It is the partial life story of a boy born in Orkney on the island of Norday, at around the same time as Mackay Brown himself: Thorfinn was old enough to be a soldier in the Second World War. But it is the partial biography of his growing imagination, rather than his school life and later career. Like the other novels, this one is rendered in episodes, but here it is the boy's vision that links these together. Characteristically, Thorfinn is a schoolboy bored with school, as indeed was Mackay Brown himself: in an early autobiographical essay he described school as 'the huge gray unimaginative machine took us and tried to mould us'.[12] Here Thorfinn starts dreaming of taking part in exciting and dramatic episodes from the history he failed to listen to in class from Mr Simon, 'about the Norsemen in Constantinople 800 years ago.' (p 1) Mr Simon dismisses him as a dreamer with neither talent nor future, who would even be useless as a soldier – 'a lazy useless boy'. Meanwhile Thorfinn in his dreaming imagination sails to Russia with a band of outlawed Swedes, saving their lives in the passing, and they reach Constantinople and join the Emperor's guard, from which Thorfinn is rescued and taken home by Earl Rognvald of Orkney.

In the second chapter there is another dream of warfare. Thorfinn goes to sleep during a political discussion at the forge and dreams of following a knight on horseback, (oddly reminiscent of Mr MacTavish, the loquacious SNP publican), on a quest to 'help the King of Scotland in his War of Independence against the King of England.' This adventure ends more ignominiously than the last, with the horse dying, worn out, and the travellers both very drunk, so that they are too late for Bannockburn. The pair are rendered self important and absurd, and the war is seen as something distant and far off that they do not figure in. Other wars figure in later episodes, but not in a traditional romantic or bloodthirsty way: in the chapter 'Broch' an early generation of settlers in the islands are saved from destruction by a later influx because of their craftiness in the invention and construction of this impregnable fortress structure, one on every island, and much is made of the mockery visited on the needy newcomers by their safe, well fed inhabitants, and Thorfinn the boy poet makes songs for their triumph.

Even in the sixth chapter, 'The Press Gang and The Seal Dance', large-scale war comes to threaten Norday only to be mocked by the wit and strategy of the inhabitants. For the last time the boy drifts off into a dream, of 'the reign of good King George III'. For the last time the islands throw off the threat: the menacing arrival of the Press Gang turns into a merry game, with the young men – and all the other islanders – duping the officers with triumphant ease, so that not a man is taken. (Thorfinn himself gives a superb performance of one dying of galloping consumption.) Meanwhile, back in the 1930s, Thorfinn leaves school at fourteen and helps his father Matthew carry on the farm. But now modern life intrudes, with the beginnings of a threat that cannot be repudiated. Matthew buys a primitive wireless set, which brings them the music of Henry Hall and the BBC Dance Orchestra and radio dramas. But,

> one night they heard a voice screaming and ranting and raging in a foreign language.[…]They found out later that it was the ruler of Germany, Adolf Hitler, saying that his patience was exhausted, that his claim to Sudetenland was the last territorial demand he had to make in Europe… Oh, it was a hideous voice, Ragna said it frightened her more – far more – than *Murder in the Red Barn*. (pp 133-4)

So now in 'real' time the islands are at last threatened by omens of large-scale warfare, however distantly. This threat is made clear before Thorfinn's last boyhood dream, and three mysterious strangers arrive and claim power over six farms and their people.

Before this, there are a few chapters *not* directly concerned with war, and it can be argued that they have key importance in the book as key moments in Thorfinn's development. In 'A Man's Life' Thorfinn encounters the fact of death for the first time. Jacob Olafson's death and life are recorded, partly in Thorfinn's dream. 'The thought that this old man was not part of the island any more, though – that filled the boy with wonderment'. (p 50) Now for the first time, sitting on the kirkyard wall, he contemplates birth and life and death:

> The life of a man, thought Thorfinn, is a brief voyage, with the ocean of eternity, the many-voiced sea, all around. (p 52)

Jacob's later life was for long years uneventful, but as a young man he ran away to Hudson's Bay the day his sister was to marry, and came back years later to the ancestral croft with a Cree bride who died giving birth to his daughter Janet. For the rest of his life he enjoyed rum and fishing in his boat *Scallop*, but was kept in order by Janet, and he died suddenly and cleanly in a healthy old age. This life is a whole story, with the dialogue rendered, unusually, in the local dialect.

Thorfinn sees it poetically, with the new-born child in 'his little ship of time, his cradle', plotting a full day's voyage until his coffin, 'Jacob Olafson's death-ship'. (p 69) Jacob's Cree wife, whom we see briefly, has a mysterious, unknowable quality about her, as does the seal-wife that an early Thorfinn marries in an earlier dream, but the most striking of the young women that figure in the book is an apparition that strikes him in his early teens, in the chapter called, plainly, 'The Muse'. This chapter is the only one without a daydream by young Thorfinn: this is real life, with a touch of inexplicable wonder, as the boy experiences the very first stirrings of love.

Sophie is the object of general speculation when she comes to stay with the bachelor minister, but she later turns out to be his step-sister. She appears to the boy when he is dreaming of the Prince, and the Flight Through the Heather:

> There, against the surging blue and white of the sky (for
> it was a windy morning) the girl who was staying at the
> minister's (whoever she was) rode the laird's chestnut, her
> yellow hair streaming out behind her. The girl and the horse
> climbed the peat track to the summit of the hill Fea. (p 93)

Carrying brightness everywhere she goes, the girl briefly blesses the island with her presence. On her last day on Norday she singles out Thorfinn and says: 'You, poet, wait for me. I'll come back some day. Never forget.' (p 125) She kisses him and leaves.

With the seventh chapter, 'The Aerodrome', war at last comes to Norday, not in the form of an invading hostile army, but in the ambiguous guise of national defence. Gradually, but quickly, six farms are commandeered, then other buildings and small businesses, until everyone is exiled. The noise is terrible: 'all this whirl of clangour, uprooting, confusion, pulverization, fire'. (p 188) Mackay Brown wrote elsewhere, 'The islands shook with Wagnerian noise.' [13] Soon the plan becomes clear:

> Now all of Norday knew what was going to happen: all that
> fertile part of the island between the hill and the shore was

> to be laid out in runways and hangars, so that the German
> bombers, if they ever flew over Scapa Flow to attack the
> battle fleet anchored there would, themselves cumbersome
> and slow, be engaged by swift leaf-light lancing fighter
> planes, the toreadors of the sky. (p 186)

People react according to their life-styles: Thomas Vass the factor –
and the incoming influx – promise money beyond islanders' dreams.
But farmers whose farms have been family-owned for hundreds
of years despair: one man burns his farm, without even thinking
of insuring it first; the inn-keeper dies of despair; young Thorfinn
Ragnarson disappears.

This is all very reminiscent of *Greenvoe*, and the clearance of the
island in the name of modern scientific installations. But the novelist
does not oppose it as that earlier novel so clearly did. The war is seen
as essential, and cannot be simply opposed, like Black Star; but the
devastation is complete. Mackay Brown's opposition to concrete and
the paraphernalia of modern times has never been bleaker, and the
fact that the novelist sees fighting the war as the lesser of two evils
makes it even more deadening.

But the hope renewed at the end of *Greenvoe* is realised much
sooner and more clearly here. The final chapter, 'Fisherman and
Croftwoman' begins the restoration, as well as telling us the ironic
story of Thorfinn's war. Thorfinn eventually returns to the island,
a published author with some success, but coming to reinhabit it,
rebuild the boat, and devote himself to land restoration, not writing.
We learn just enough about his war, which was inglorious enough.
He spent it in captivity, having been captured soon after Dunkirk,
and latterly had a good time in a Bavarian prison camp: he happened
on a German officer who encouraged his attempt to write the stories
of his early dreams and even lent him a typewriter, so that by the
time he was freed he had written two romances, versions of the first
two dreams the boy experiences in this book. Later in Edinburgh he
writes more. There is a version of 'Broch', and then we meet again
the shade of *Greenvoe*:

And then this hack historian had a great breakthrough. He tried something different – the impact on a primitive simple society, close to the elements, of a massive modern technology. He had experienced it at first hand, in his native island, when that pastoral place had been almost overnight changed into a fortress in the months before the Second World War. (p 214)

This novel, 'not historical but throwing a cold shadow into the future,' is an immediate success. Thorfinn goes back alone to Norday, dissatisfied with his work, which in his eyes lacked 'the innocent poetry of the first imagining'. (p 215) He tells all this to Sophie, miraculously arrived on the island the year before, and their coming together forms a satisfactory happy ending. He belittles the possibility of achieving his dream of real writing, and professes the wish to farm and fish: perhaps, says Sophie, their son will be the poet.

The novel deserves its place as treating the Second World War in its impact on the way of life he describes above: there are wartime airfields still, in Orkney. It is an effective protest at the destructiveness of this war in terms of civilian life, without ever questioning its necessity.

NOTES

1. See *Scottish Writers Talking 1*, ed, Isobel Murray, Kennedy & Boyd, Glasgow, 2008.

2. See '*The Broken Heraldry*' in Karl Miller, ed, *Memoirs of a Modern Scotland*, London, 1970, p 139.

3. *Maggie Fergusson, George Mackay Brown: The Life*, London, 2006, pp 44–6.

4. See Isobel Murray and Bob Tait, *Ten Modern Scottish Novels*, Aberdeen, 1984, p 149.

5. See *For the Islands I Sing: An Autobiography*, London, 1997, p 173.

6. *Scottish Writers Talking 1*, p 47.

7. *Ten Modern Scottish Novels*, pp 144-167.

8. *Scottish Writers Talking 1*, p 23.

9. See Julian Meldon D'Arcy, *Scottish Skalds and Sagamen: Old Norse Influence on Modern Scottish Literature*, East Linton, 1996, pp 242–83.

10. *Scottish Writers Talking 1*, p 44.

11. *Scottish Writers Talking 1*, p 22. See also Fergusson, pp 222–3.

12. See Maurice Lindsay, ed, *As I Remember: Ten Scottish Authors Recall How for Them Writing Began*, London, 1979, p 19.

13. *For the Islands I Sing*, p 59.

LIST OF NOVELS CONSULTED

See below for a list of novelists engaging to some extent with the war, and their books:

(James BARKE 1905–1958
Warnings:
| 1936 | *Major Operation* |
| 1939 | *Land of the Leal*) |

George Mackay BROWN 1921–1996
1972	*Greenvoe*
1973	*Magnus*
1984	*Time in a Red Coat*
1994	*Beside the Ocean of Time*

James Allan FORD 1920–2009
| 1961 | *The Brave White Flag* |
| 1963 | *Season of Escape* |

(George Macdonald FRASER 1925–2007
No novels about World War Two, but a masterly memoir:
| 1992 | *Quartered Safe Out Here*) |

Catherine GAVIN 1907–2000
1976	*Traitor's Gate*
1977	*None Dare Call It Treason*
1980	*How Sleep the Brave*

(Lewis Grassic GIBBON 1901–35
Warnings:
1934   *Grey Granite*)

Stuart HOOD 1915–
1955   *Since the Fall*
1963/1984 *Pebbles From my Skull/Carlino*
1987   *The Upper Hand*
1991   *A Den of Foxes*

Robin JENKINS 1912–2005
1956   *Guests of War*
1979   *Fergus Lamont*
1988   *Just Duffy*

Jessie KESSON 1916–1994
1983   *Another Time, Another Place*

John KOVACK/Neil PATERSON: *See under Paterson*

Eric LINKLATER 1899–1974
1946   *Private Angelo*
1955   *The Dark of Summer*
1961   *Roll of Honour*

Compton MACKENZIE 1883–1972
1943   *Keep the Home Guard Turning* (one of the
            Monarch of the Glen series of Highland comedies)

Moray McLAREN 1901–71
1947   *Escape and Return* 'lower bohemian London
            during the air-raids' Very little on this: mostly 'war
            weariness, breakdown and searching for faith'.
            A first novel.

Alistair MacLEAN 1922–87
   1955   *HMS Ulysses*
                And many more!

Allan Campbell MacLEAN 1922–1989
   1969   *The Glasshouse*

(Ian MACPHERSON 1905–44
   1935   *Wild Harbour*)

Bruce MARSHALL 1899–1987
   1954   *Only Fade Away*
   1972   *The Black Oxen*

Naomi MITCHISON 1897–1999
   1939   *The Blood of the Martyrs*
   1947   *The Bull Calves*
   1957   *Five Men and a Swan*
   1960   *The Rib of the Green Umbrella* for children

Nancy Brysson MORRISON 1907–86
   1957   *The Other Traveller*
                (a dead war hero important here)

Neil PATERSON/John KOVACK 1916–1995
   1949   *On My Faithless Arm* by 'John Kovack'.
                First novel.

John PREBBLE 1915–2001
   1943   *Where the Sea Breaks*
   1948   *The Edge of Darkness*

Jack RONDER 1924–1979
   1977   *Mouse Code* (for children) - about Gruinard and anthrax
   1978   *The Lost Tribe*

Archie ROY 1924 –

1970   *All Evil Shed Away*

J D SCOTT 1917–1980

1947/48   *The Cellar/Buy It for a Song*

1954   *The End of an Old Song*

Muriel SPARK 1918–2006

1963   *The Girls of Slender Means*

1974   *The Hothouse by the East River*

Nigel TRANTER 1909–2000

1944   *Delayed Action*

Fred URQUHART 1912–95

1949   *The Ferret Was Abraham's Daughter*

1951   *Jezebel's Dust*

James WOOD 1918 – unknown

1959   *The Sealer*

Oswald WYND 1913–98

1947   *Black Fountains*

1972   *The Forty Days*

GENERAL BIBLIOGRAPHY
BOOKS

W R AITKEN, *Scottish Literature in English and Scots: A Guide to Information Sources*, Detroit, 1982.

Carol ANDERSON and Aileen CHRISTIANSON, eds, *Scottish Women's Fiction, 1920s to 1960s: Journeys into Being*, East Linton, 2000.

Jill BENTON, *Naomi Mitchison: A Biography: A Century of Experiment in Life and Letters*, London, 1990.

Alan BOLD, *Modern Scottish Literature*, London, 1983.

Ray BRADFIELD, *Nigel Tranter: Scotland's Storyteller*, Edinburgh, 1999.

George Mackay BROWN, *For The Islands I Sing: An Autobiography*, London, 1997.

Moyra BURGESS, *Imagine a City: Glasgow in fiction*, Glendaruel, 1998.

Angus CALDER, *The People's War: Britain 1939-45*, London, 1969.

Angus CALDER, *Scotlands of the Mind*, Edinburgh, 2002.

Jenni CALDER, *The Nine Lives of Naomi Mitchison*, London, 1997.

Cairns CRAIG, *The Modern Scottish Novel*, Edinburgh, 1999.

Cairns CRAIG, *Out of History: Narrative Paradigms in Scottish and British Culture*, Edinburgh, 1996.

Julian Meldon D'ARCY, *Skalds and Sagamen: Old Norse Influence in Modern Scottish Literature*, East Linton, 1996.

Maggie FERGUSSON, *George Mackay Brown: The Life*, London, 2006.

George MacDonald FRASER, *Quartered Safe Out Here: A Recollection of the War in Burma*, London, 1993.

Paul FUSSELL, *Wartime: Understanding and Behaviour in the Second World War*, New York and Oxford, 1989.

Douglas GIFFORD and Dorothy McMILLAN, eds, *A History of Scottish Women's Writing*, Edinburgh, 1997.

Martin GILBERT, *Second World War*, New Edition, London, 2003.

David HEWITT, ed, *Northern Visions: The Literary Identity of Northern Scotland in the Twentieth Century*, East Linton, 1995.

Maurice LINDSAY, ed, *As I Remember: Ten Scottish Authors Recall How Writing Began for Them*, London, 1979.

Andro LINKLATER, *Compton Mackenzie: A Life*, London, 1987.

Eric LINKLATER, *Fanfare for a Tin Hat: A Third Essay in Autobiography*, London, 1970.

Norman LONGMATE, *How We Lived Then: A History of Everyday Life During the Second World War*, London, 1971.

Ian MacDOUGALL, ed, *Voices from War: Personal Recollections of War in our Century by Scottish Men and Women*, Edinburgh, 1995.

Karl MILLER, ed, *Memoirs of a Modern Scotland*, London, 1970.

Naomi MITCHISON, *You May Well Ask: A Memoir 1920–1940*, London, 1979.

Isobel MURRAY, ed, *Beyond This Limit: Selected Shorter Fiction of Naomi Mitchison*, Glasgow, 2008.

Isobel MURRAY, ed, *Scottish Writers Talking 1*, Kennedy and Boyd, Glasgow, 2008.

Isobel MURRAY, ed, *Scottish Writers Talking 2*, East Linton, 2002.

Isobel MURRAY, ed, *Scottish Writers Talking 3*, Edinburgh, 2006.

Isobel MURRAY, ed, *Scottish Writers Talking 4*, Kennedy and Boyd, Glasgow, 2009.

Isobel MURRAY and Bob TAIT, *Ten Modern Scottish Novels*, Aberdeen, 1984.

Gill PLAIN, *Women's Fiction of the Second World War: Gender, Power and Resistance*, Edinburgh, 1996.

Anne POWELL, ed, *Shadows of War: British Women's Poetry of the Second World War*, Stroud, 1999.

Trevor ROYLE, *The Mainstream Companion to Scottish Literature*, Edinburgh, 1993.

Joachim SCHWEND and Horst DRESCHER, eds, *Studies in Scottish Fiction: Twentieth Century*, Frankfurt am Main, 1990.

Elaine SHOWALTER, *The Female Malady: Women, Madness and English Culture 1830–1980*, London, 1987.

Muriel SPARK, *Curriculum Vitae: Autobiography*, London, 1992.

Gavin WALLACE and Randall STEVENSON, eds, *The Scottish Novel Since the Seventies: New Visions, Old Dreams*, Edinburgh, 1993.

Norman WILSON, ed, *Scottish Writing and Writers*, Edinburgh, 1977.

ARTICLES AND CONTRIBUTIONS TO BOOKS

Ian CAMPBELL, 'Beside Brown's Ocean of Time' in Susanne Hagemann, ed, *Studies in Scottish Fiction: 1945 to the Present*, Frankfurt am Main, 1996, pp 263–274.

Cairns CRAIG, 'Robin Jenkins – A Would-be Realist?' in *Edinburgh Review* 106, pp 12–22.

Douglas GIFFORD, 'Literature and World War Two' in Ian Brown and Alan Riach, eds, *The Edinburgh Companion to Twentieth-Century Scottish Literature*, Edinburgh, 2009, pp 88–102.

Bob LUMLEY, 'Keeping Faith: an Interview with Stuart Hood', *Edinburgh Review* 79/80, 1988, pp 172–206.

Hugh MacPHERSON, 'Fred Urquhart' in *The Scottish Book-Collector*, February/March 1992, pp 27–30.

Isobel MURRAY, '"Clemency Ealasaid July 1940": The Turning Point in a Poet's War' in *Scottish Studies Review*, Volume 6, No 2, Autumn, 2005, pp 72–83.

Isobel MURRAY, 'Novelists of the Renaissance' in Cairns Craig, ed, *The History of Scottish Literature Volume 4: Twentieth Century*, Aberdeen, 1987, pp103–117.

Isobel MURRAY, 'The White Bird Passes: How Jessie Kesson Reached the Final Version' in *Scottish Studies Review*, Volume 7, No 1, Spring, 2006, pp 68–79.

Bob TAIT, 'Introduction' to Canongate Classics edition of Robin Jenkins' *Fergus Lamont*, 1990.

Fred URQUHART, 'Forty-Three Years: A Benediction', in *The Ghost of Liberace, New Writing Scotland No 11*, 1993, pp 135–146.